A MANUAL

OF

MARITIME LAW.

CONSISTING OF

A TREATISE ON SHIPS AND FREIGHT

AND

A TREATISE ON INSURANCE.

TRANSLATED FROM THE LATIN OF ROCCUS.

WITH NOTES.

BY JOSEPH REED INGERSOLL.

The Maritime Law is not the law of a particular country, *but the general law of nations.*　　　　　Lord Mansfield.

THE LAWBOOK EXCHANGE, LTD.
Clark, New Jersey

ISBN-13: 9781584778318 (hardcover)
ISBN-13: 9781616190460 (paperback)

Lawbook Exchange edition 2010

The quality of this reprint is equivalent to the quality of the original work.

THE LAWBOOK EXCHANGE, LTD.
33 Terminal Avenue
Clark, New Jersey 07066-1321

*Please see our website for a selection of our other publications
and fine facsimile reprints of classic works of legal history:*
www.lawbookexchange.com

Library of Congress Cataloging-in-Publication Data

Rocco, Francesco, 1605-1676.
  A manual of maritime law, consisting of a treatise on ships
and freight and a treatise on insurance / translated from the
Latin of Roccus with notes by Joseph Reed Ingersoll.
        p. cm.
  Originally published: Philadelphia : Hopkins and Earle, 1809.
  Includes bibliographical references and index.
  ISBN-13: 978-1-58477-831-8 (cloth : alk. paper)
  ISBN-10: 1-58477-831-8 (cloth : alk. paper)
  1. Maritime law. 2. Insurance, Marine. I. Ingersoll, Joseph R.
(Joseph Reed), 1786-1868. II. Title.
  K1155.R63 2007
  343.09'6--dc22   2007004132

Printed in the United States of America on acid-free paper

A MANUAL

OF

MARITIME LAW.

CONSISTING OF

A TREATISE ON SHIPS AND FREIGHT

AND

A TREATISE ON INSURANCE.

TRANSLATED FROM THE LATIN OF ROCCUS.

WITH NOTES.

BY JOSEPH REED INGERSOLL.

The Maritime Law is not the law of a particular country, *but the general law of nations.* Lord Mansfield.

PHILADELPHIA:

PUBLISHED BY HOPKINS AND EARLE
Fry and Kammerer, Printers.
1809.

PREFACE.

THE works of Roccus, though of great celebrity, are read only by the professed civilian. The ensuing treatises contain principles of utility to the merchant and the mariner, yet they are known to them only through the medium of quotations scattered through a great variety of later authors. The excellence of the work is sufficiently manifested by the respect with which its author is uniformly noticed, and the confidence with which his opinions are cited by almost every writer on the same subject, since his time. It has been thought advisable to unlock the stores which have been heretofore concealed from those for whom they were intended, and to present to the American merchant the Treatises of Roccus, in an English dress.

FRANCESCO ROCCI, or ROCCUS, as he is commonly called, by affixing a Latin termination to his

name, according to the custom of the learned in former ages, was an eminent jurist of the city of Naples, and one of the judges of the *Magna Curia*, or
supreme court of that kingdom. He flourished about
the middle of the seventeenth century, and his two
treatises, *on ships and freight*, and *on insurance*,
were first published at Naples in the year 1655.
Since that period, several editions have been printed
in various parts of the continent of Europe; among
these, one of the most esteemed is the edition published at Amsterdam in the year 1708, by the learned *Westerween*, from which the following translation has been made.

Besides these two tracts on which our author's
fame principally rests, he has published two hundred opinions on various questions of jurisprudence,
from which his Dutch editor, *Westerween*, has select-
ed fourteen, relative to subjects of maritime law,
which are printed at the end of his volume, under
the title of *Selecta Responsa*. They are remarkable
for the same sound logic, depth of learning, and dis-
criminating acumen, by which the rest of his works
are so eminently distinguished.

The law which regulates insurance, and the other branches of maritime commerce is not peculiar to any particular nation. To this law, lord Mansfield has with great propriety applied the words of Tully: *Non erit lex alia Romæ, alia Athenis, alia nunc, alia posthac, sed et omni tempore, et apud omnes gentes, una eademque lex obtinebit.* * The Roman emperor Antoninus declared that although he was master of the world, yet the maritime law was sovereign of the sea.† This principle is recognised by all the commercial nations of Europe, who for the purposes of trade, consider themselves as one great family, governed and regulated by the same system of laws. Hence with few variations the same principles and the same rules, which regulate the decisions of the courts of Great Britain and of the United States, are to be found in the earliest treatises on maritime law. For these, next to the Rhodians whose commercial regulations are in part preserved in the imperial

---

* There shall not be one law at Rome, and another at Athens, one law now, and another hereafter, but among all nations and at all times, one and the same law shall prevail. *Cic. Fragm. de Repub.* quoted by lord Mansfield in *Luke & al.* v. *Lyde*, 2 *Bur.* 887.

† See the note to Note XLVIII. in our author's Treatise on Ships and Freight.

B

code of Rome, we are chiefly indebted to the writers
of Italy and Spain, where commerce was first re-
vived after the destruction of the western empire.
To them we owe the celebrated work of the *Consolato*, for which those two nations are still contending.
Insurance and bills of exchange were first introduced into the rest of Europe by the Italian merchants,
who were at that time denominated *Lombards*. And
to this day, a clause still introduced into English
policies of assurance points to the source, whence
England first derived her knowledge of commercial
law.‡ Numerous works were published in Spain
and Italy at an early period to elucidate this interesting branch of knowledge. Among them no one
is considered of greater weight than the work now
offered to the public.

- . The treatises of Roccus are remarkable for their
brevity. They do not, like the modern essays of
Abbott, Park, and Marshall, or Valin, Pothier, and
Emerigon, pretend to enter into a minute description of every case, but like the Tenures of Lyttleton

‡ *This writing or policy of assurance shall be of as much force
and effect as the surest writing or policy of assurance heretofore
made in* LOMBARD STREET *or elsewhere.*

they embrace in the abstract, principles that are ca-
pable of an extension not less wide than the Com-
mentaries of Sir Edward Coke. Unembarrassed by
tedious annotations, they are designed as a manual,
to the advocate who will find here many important
principles of his science, and will turn with facility
to the useful remarks of " this learned civilian;" to
the merchant whose intelligence will be increased,
and whose litigation will be prevented by a frequent
recurrence to our author; and to the mariner, who
will be in possession of a compendium of principles,
useful in his profession.

From a national pride and prejudice, and from a
reluctance to acknowledge their obligations to foreign writers, the English civilians have suffered most
of the learned treatises on maritime law, to remain in
a dead language, accessible only to the scholar, and
hidden from the class of individuals to whom they
are of chief importance. We confidently trust that
the liberality of an American public will delight to
encourage the extension of science, whether derived
from Naples or Genoa, from Barcelona or from
Rome. Even in England the prejudice to which we
allude is rapidly diminishing; and modern writers

and judges do not hesitate to receive from foreign
sources, those lights which cannot be obtained elsewhere.

In the ensuing translation, little merit is claimed,
but that of accuracy. The object has been to render
the author's meaning as clear as possible without
an attempt at ornament. If this humble effort has met
with success, no contemptible service will be rendered to the public, and no unworthy addition made to
the library of the professional or mercantile reader.
We have endeavoured to pursue the plan and manner of the original as nearly as possible, without fal-
ling into an imitation so servile as to render the
phraseology awkward or the meaning obscure.
Where, for instance, technical terms or ordinary ex-
pressions have varied from a literal translation, they
have been adopted without hesitation. And in some
instances where a sentence or even an entire *note*,
has been found totally inapplicable to our law, and
at the same time devoid of interest in itself, it has
been omitted. But in general it will be found that
few deviations are made from a course of expression, which we presume the author himself would

have employed, had he written in the English language.

If the shortness of the work create an opinion unfavourable to its value, it will at least form an apology for intruding on public notice, as little time will be required for the perusal. And if any merit should appear, let this be considered an introduction to the jurist, with whose writings, the reader at a future period may be made better acquainted.

The original title of the book is *Notabilia de Navibus et Naulo, item de Assecurationibus*, or *Remarks on Ships and Freight, and on Insurance*. It is divided into *centuries*, each treatise consisting of one hundred articles which are headed N o т. I. II. III. &c. These subdivisions have therefore been called *notes* by the English writers in their quotations from this work. Lord Mansfield in the celebrated case of *Luke et al.* v. *Lyde,* 2 *Burr.* 889. refers to *Roccus on Ships and Freight,* N o т е 81. In the report of the same case in 1 *Bl. Rep.* 191. the reference is to Num° 81. But in *Marshall on Insurance, Abbott on Shipping*, and the generality of English writers by whom our author is quoted, the divisions are called N o т е s.

and are referred to by that name. It has therefore
been adopted in this translation. The opinions or
Responsa of Roccus, are also divided into *centuries*,
consisting as we have said, of two hundred articles,
one hundred of which are classed under each century. This seems to have been the fashion of the
times. Jenkins who wrote in England, in the reign
of James I. published his reports in the form of centuries.

Our author supports his opinions by an immense
number of references and quotations, the greater
part of which, it has been thought proper to omit.
The opinions themselves having stood the test of
ages, are now authorities of infinitely greater weight
than the writers from whom they are quoted. Many
of these are scarcely known by name,* and their
works have never reached America. Some of these
quotations however, have been preserved, particularly in the treatise on ships and freight, where we

* Such for instance as, *L. Cardinalis, Fontanella, S. Oddus,
A. de Ansaldis, M. Giurba, A. de Velasco, P. P. Corneus, R.
Suarius, N. Boerius, H. Rocca, H. Leotardus, A. Gamma, L.
Lopes, F. de Roxa, J. Giballinus, S. de Homodeis, J. F. Sanfeli-
cius, M. de Afflictis, G. Mastrillus, L. Molina, P. N. Mossius.
J. D. Gaitus,* and many others.

have thought they might lead the reader to a further
investigation of the subject. In that treatise we have
preserved most of the references to the body of
the civil law, the principal source of legal learning
on the continent of Europe, from which the common law itself has borrowed many important principles. We have preserved some citations from
Straccha, and the decisions of the *Court of Rota of
Genoa*, and not a few from the work of *John de Hevia*, which deserves to be better known.

At the conclusion of most of the *notes*, we have
inserted the names of one or more English or
American writers by whom the opinion of Roccus
there expressed has been quoted; and of adjudged
cases, in which the decision has been partly founded
upon his authority. Writers of eminent respecta-
bility only, have been chosen, although further re-
search would have found the name of Roccus, used
in many books of inferior reputation. We have been
induced to do this, that the weight and influence of
our author's sentiments may appear by the frequent
references made to him by writers of acknowledged
merit; and that the reader may be directed to the
passages in these standard authorities, where the sub-

ject is more fully treated of, and more completely displayed.

In the quotations from *Straccha*, from the *Corpus Juris Civilis*, and from other writers, a translation merely is inserted, to avoid swelling the notes with the original texts. The references however are so made that the reader may turn without difficulty to the works themselves and judge of the accuracy of our translation.

It is certainly much to be desired that the treatises of law, and particularly those connected with commerce, should be of easy access to all who are interested in them. To this end, labour would be well bestowed; and our country might claim no humble praise for having preserved the works of legal science which time had obscured or prejudice neglected, and introduced them again into familiar use.

TREATISE

ON

SHIPS AND FREIGHT.

NOTE I.

SHIPPING and navigation, are of the greatest importance and utility to mankind. Our object in these notes is to explain the general rules and principles of law, by which they are regulated.

NOTE II.

Freight is the consideration or premium promised to the master of a ship for carrying goods or persons from one place to another.

NOTE III.

The master of the vessel is he, to whom the care of the vessel is entirely confided. To his charge and direction the whole of the ship and every thing that

C

belongs to her, and the mariners are committed. He may be a freeman, a minor, or a slave. There may be one, or two masters at the pleasure of the owner, which may be either express or implied. *John de Hevia, lib.* 3. *cap.* 4. *n.* 2. He alone is not the master to whom the owner has confided the command of the ship, but he also to whom this master has intrusted the authority, may officiate as commander whether the owners were acquainted with the circumstance or not. *Dig. lib.* 14. *tit.* 1. *l.* 1. § 5.

Quoted in *Abbott,* 78.

NOTE IV.

If in consequence of any accident the ship be deprived of her master, the mariners may nominate and elect a commander, when they are in a place where the owners cannot make the nomination. *John de Hevia, lib.* 3. *cap.* 4. *n.* 2. (*a*)

(*a*) *John de Hevia Bolanos,* is a Spanish writer of eminence and the author of an excellent treatise on the laws of Spain, entitled *Curia Philipica.* The third book of this work, to which our author frequently refers, is devoted to the subject of maritime jurisprudence.

NOTE V.

The master of a ship nominated and appointed by the owner, may substitute another commander in his place *though forbidden by the owner.* (*b*) *John de Hevia, lib.* 3. *cap.* 4. *n.* 2. *Dig. lib.* 14. *tit.* 1. *l.* 5.

NOTE VI.

If a ship have two owners who cannot agree in the choice of a commander, and therefore make different nominations, in this case as *several* concur in granting an *indivisible* right to *different* persons they interfere with one another and no effect is produced. That nomination however is preferred which will afford the better commander. But if both of the owners choose a competent person, and still cannot agree, the Judge should interpose and endeavour to persuade them to an agreement; and if the Judge

(*b*) This is to be understood merely as to the contracts made by freighters or other third persons with the deputy so appointed, but not so as to discharge the master from his responsibility to the owner if he should disobey his orders. "*He who has appointed a master,*" says the text of the civil law quoted by our author, "*must answer for all his acts, otherwise they who contract might be deceived.*"

cannot effect a concurrence, the ship must remain
without a commander until a concurrent appointment
can be made.

NOTE VII.

Two owners of a ship, equally interested in her,
may appoint the commander alternately every year:
but if they are entitled to unequal proportions, each
must choose the master for a period proportioned to
his interest in the vessel.

John de Hevia observes that as any person may be
a master of a ship, he ought to be an able seaman,
and undergo a regular examination: he should also
be a native of the kingdom; a foreigner, indeed, may
be appointed where no native can be obtained, but
he should be careful in his command to observe the
laws of Spain. (*c*) Nor should he be a person of in-
different character, for he is considered in the light
of a soldier, and enjoys military privileges. (*d*) *John
de Hevia, lib. 3. cap. 4.*

(*c*) The kingdom of Naples at the time when our author
wrote, was under the dominion of the crown of Spain.

(*d*) This is well calculated for the encouragement of commerce and navigation under a military government.

NOTE VIII.

The master of the ship has power to confine of-
fenders in the vessel, even though they are not mariners, for the purpose of delivering them up to the
competent authority of the territory or district nearest to the place where the offence was committed.
Or he may confine them in port where the ship is
to be unladen, in order to have them punished. On
the other hand, if the master of the ship be guilty of
an offence, any of the sailors may put him in con-
finement and deliver him to a competent authority.
John de Hevia, lib. 3. § 11. *n.* 6.

Quoted in *Abbott,* 109.

NOTE IX.

(*e*) *The pilot* is he who directs the *sailing* of the
vessel, and he is supposed to be perfectly acquainted
with navigation. The pilot is chosen by the master
of the ship and is responsible for every injury occasioned by his fault, ignorance or negligence in the
government of the vessel; he is liable for the most

(*e*) The *pilot* on board of Spanish vessels, is the same as our
mate, with a more honourable title.

trifling fault that shews a deviation from the strictest
attention to his duty.

The *clerk* or *purser*, is a person appointed by the
master, who is bound to take care of the *ship's books*,
in which every thing on board is inserted, as well
the names of the mariners as the articles of merchandize shipped. He is bound to describe them *minutely*,
in manner and form as they were taken on board.
He is therefore in some measure considered a public
officer.

Mariner, is a term of extensive import, and comprehends all persons who *do duty* on board of the
ship, and are instrumental to her navigation. They
are also chosen by the master.

NOTE X.

A master of a ship may be compelled to sail with
his ship and to carry goods, passengers and sailors,
and to make any *ordinary voyage*, because the public good requires it, and the public have a right to
the use of ships. So widely is this principle extended
that if a person endeavour to excuse his ship from
public use, (*f*) it will be confiscated. Another reason

(*f*) This law was established towards the end of the fourth

for this principle is, that the owner or master of a ship is considered in the light of an innkeeper, who, after opening his house and undertaking to entertain, may be compelled regularly to receive guests.

NOTE XI.

The owner of a vessel is responsible for the contracts and the criminal acts of the master appointed by him. He is responsible also for the *faults* of the mariners committed at sea, but not for their *contracts*, as they were appointed by the master of the ship and not by him. *Dig. lib.* 14. *tit.* 1. § 5. (*g*) It is different therefore in the case of *contracts* and *crimes*. The owner is bound by every act of the master, but only by the fraud or faults or crimes of the sailors.

century by the Roman emperors, *Arcadius*, and *Honorius*, and may be considered as the origin of *impressments*. See *Justinian's Code, lib.* xi. *tit.* 3. *De Navibus non excusandis.*

(*g*) Our author means here by *criminal acts*, those only which relate to navigation, and are committed by the master and mariners in violation of their duty as such, and so indeed he explains his meaning at the end of the note. By saying that the owner of a ship is responsible for such acts committed by the captain or crew, he means *civilly*, not *criminally*. That is to say, he is responsible for the loss which such acts may occasion to the shippers. Such is our law.

If a servant be guilty of any improprieties in the office or employment assigned him by his master, the master is answerable for such improprieties, as he should not have employed such a servant, and the fault may therefore be imputed to him. Nor in the instance above mentioned, will the owner be excused by delivering up the master or sailors; for the case is like that of an innkeeper, where it is not sufficient to deliver up the offender, but the party sustaining a loss has his election whether to proceed against the master or the servant.

The above principle is applicable only to offences affecting articles on board of the ship and belonging to her, and committed by sailors in the vessel: it does not extend to crimes committed out of the ship.

Quoted in *Abbott*, 79. 2 *Browne's Civ. & Adm. Law*, 157.

NOTE XII.

If the master of a vessel exceed his orders, for example, if he have instructions from his owners to obtain freight, and not to charter the ship generally, and afterwards he charters her, the owner is not responsible. Or if the owners direct him to carry passengers, and not to load the ship with goods, and he disregards their orders, they are not liable. If the master be directed to load the ship with a particular sort of goods, for instance, with grain, and he loads her with marble, or any other article, the owners are not bound. *Dig. lib.* 14. *tit.* 1. *l.* 1. § 12. (*h*) A master of a vessel was directed not to ship Venetian goods; in opposition to which orders, he received the goods of a certain Venetian on board, which were embezzled by the sailors: although by the court of admiralty the owners were decreed to pay the loss, yet by the superior tribunal this decree was reversed.

Quoted in *Abbott*, 79.

(*h*) The text of the civil law to which our author refers, puts the case of a son, who having a general authority from his father, to sell and dispose of all his property, makes a fraudulent sale thereof, for his own benefit. Such a sale, says the Digest, is not binding upon the father, notwithstanding the general words of the authority. But the Digest means no more than that the sale is not binding as between the father and son, nor with respect to the purchaser, if he were a party to the fraud. In every other point of view, it is to be considered as valid. Our author undoubtedly does not mean to carry this doctrine any farther. See *Abbott*, 78.

D

NOTE XIII.

The owners are not liable for the faults of a master who exceeds his instructions, even though the instructions were general; for *faults* are never comprehended in such general instructions. *Dig. lib.* 17. *tit.* 1. *l.* 60. § 4. If a servant at an inn wound any person, the innkeeper is not answerable for the injury or expenses. So if a child or slave commit a crime, in the presence of his father or master, the father or master is not responsible for the crime. So a master is not answerable, if his servant set fire to the house.

Quoted in *Abbott*, 79.

NOTE XIV.

Further, the owner is not responsible for an injury done to any one by his sailors, contrary to his *express orders*. But if this prohibition were not *express*, the owners would be liable for the crimes, deceit, and faults of the sailors, though not for their contracts, as we have said before. In no case is the owner answerable for the *contracts* of the sailors; but it is otherwise with their *crimes*, for he is bound to take care that they commit none. *Dig. lib.* 14. *tit.* 1. *l.* 1. § 1, 2, 3, 4, 5. (*i*)

Quoted in *Abbott*, 79.

NOTE XV.

If the master of a ship were appointed for a certain voyage, or for a certain place, and he proceeds on another voyage, the owners are not liable. *Ibid.* § 12.

Quoted in *Abbott*, 79.

NOTE XVI.

If several masters are appointed *generally*, without separating their authority, the command is considered as given to them all in common, so that the act of any one shall bind the owner. But if each one be invested with a distinct authority, so that one, for example, shall *contract for* the freights, and another to *receive* them, the owner is responsible for the acts of each in his own department. But if their authority

(*i*) As navigation, under the Romans, was carried on chiefly by slaves, they were considered in a measure as cattle, and therefore the owners and masters of ships were bound to keep a strict watch over them, and were held on that account to a severe responsibility. See however Note XI. in which this responsibility is restricted to offences committed *in the ship*.

be joint and not several, the owner is not answerable
for the acts of *one* alone. *Ibid.* § 13.

Quoted in *Abbott*, 79.

NOTE XVII.

The foregoing principle must be taken with this
limitation: that the owner will be responsible in the
cases mentioned, even if the master exceed his instructions, or act contrary to orders, or commit a
crime, provided the owner is benefitted by such act.
Dig. lib. 43. *tit.* 16. *l.* 1.

Quoted in *Abbott*, 79.

NOTE XVIII.

It must be observed also, that the owner is always
liable in case of theft or robbery committed by the
master, because it is always understood that the master shall not commit theft or robbery, and therefore
as he is guilty of a crime in the very essence of his
office, the owner is liable, although his instructions
may have been exceeded, or his orders disobeyed.
Dig. lib. 39. *tit.* 4. *l.* 1.

Quoted in *Abbott*, 79.

NOTE XIX.

If goods arrive in the destined port in a wet or
damaged condition, the master is liable, because he
promised in the bill of lading to deliver them, *in
like good order, and well conditioned:* particularly if
the injury arose in consequence of the ship's wanting
repairs, and the master's neglect to make them. This
fact may be easily ascertained; for if the ship were
out of repair at the time she sailed, and also at the
time of her arrival at the port of delivery, it is a na-
tural presumption that she wanted repairs during the
intermediate time while on her voyage. *Stracch. de
Nav. p.* 2. *No.* 11. *Cod. lib.* 10. *tit.* 22. *l.* 3. *Dig. lib.*
20. *tit.* 6. *l.* 8. § 7.

Quoted in *Abbott,* 146.

NOTE XX.

When a ship is purchased " *with the appurtenances*" the boat is not included; for the boat is not
an appurtenance of the ship, but is itself a small
vessel. This is so well understood, that when *a ship*
is confiscated, the boat being a separate article, is
not considered as confiscated also, for penal laws are
to be construed strictly. *Dig. lib.* 21. *tit.* 2. *l.* 44.

Ibid. lib. 6. *tit.* 1. *l.* 3. § 1. *Stracch. de Nav. p.* 1. *No.* 21.

Quoted in *Abbott*, 19.

NOTE XXI.

If a boat be overset in carrying goods from the vessel for the purpose of lightening her, a contribution is made for the benefit of the owner of the goods lost, in the same manner as if they had been thrown overboard to lighten the ship. This contribution is made by the property which remains safe on board. But if the boat with part of the goods remain safe, and the ship perish, contribution is not made for the benefit of those who lost their property in the ship. *Stracch. tit. de Nav. par.* 2. *n.* 19. *Dig. lib.* 14. *tit.* 2. *l.* 4.

NOTE XXII.

A ship often requires repairs. If one of two owners neglect or refuse to make these repairs, and the other make them himself, and the party neglecting or refusing, do not remunerate his partner in four months, with interest, for his share of the expense, he forfeits his title to the part he owned of the vessel. (*k*)

(*k*) This is a harsh law, and certainly is not in force among

NOTE XXIII.

When any person lends money to the master of a ship, for the purpose of refitting her, or to purchase articles necessary for the voyage, or to pay the sailor's wages, or to arm and equip the vessel, the owners are always liable for the debt. (*l*) But four things are requisite to render the owners liable for money so

(*l*) By the general maritime law, every contract with the master of a ship implies an hypothecation. *Justin* v. *Ballam*, 2 Lord *Raymond*, 806. But it is not so with us, and a special instrument is required. But what if a contract were made abroad with foreigners, ignorant of our local institutions; would the lien created by the operation of the general maritime law, not merely considered as such, but also as a part of the *lex loci*, be respected and enforced here? This is an important question, which we will not presume to decide: we will merely show how it has been determined abroad. *Casaregis*, an Italian writer of very great celebrity, mentions a decision at Genoa, " that a lien which is acquired on goods or effects in a foreign territory follows the property, though it be carried into another country subject to a different jurisdiction." *Casareg. Il cambista instruita, p.* 132.

Since writing this note we have found that the above principle has been adopted by the court of chancery in England, in the case of *Hussey* v. *Christie*, 13 *Ves.* junior, 594. on the authority of *Ex parte Shanks*, 1 *Atk.* 234. and of *Watkinson* v. *Bernardiston*, 2 *P. Wms.* 367. The court of Chancery in England has admiralty jurisdiction. *The King* v. *Carew*, 1 *Vern.* 54. *Gilb. Rep. in Eq. & Exch.* 227. Its decisions are authoritative therefore, we presume, in admiralty cases.

lent. *First,* The occasion must be proper, and the money must actually be expended for that purpose: yet, the lender is not bound to prove explicitly that the money was so expended. *Second,* The lender should know that the master possessed regular authority. *Third,* No greater sum should be loaned than is necessary to refit the ship, or for any other purpose. *Fourth,* The articles required must be such as can be procured in the place where the loan was made. *John de Hevia in Cur. Phil. book 3. cap. 4. n. 7. Dig. lib. 14. tit. 1. l. 7.*

NOTE XXIV.

It must be observed however, that if the master of a vessel deceive the person who lends him money, either in the repairs of the ship or the price of the articles purchased, the loss must fall on the owner, and not on the lender. If the master borrow money of another person to pay him who had advanced sums to refit the ship, still the owner is reponsible, for the new creditor is considered as having lent the money to repair the vessel.

So if a master convert to his own use, money loaned for the use of the ship, action will lie against the owner; for it is his own fault that he appointed an improper commander. *John de Hevia in Cur. Phil. book* 3. *cap.* 4. *n.* 27. *Dig. lib.* 14. *tit.* 1. *l.* 1. § 9.

NOTE XXV.

If a minor or a slave own a ship, and appoint the master, is the father or master liable for the contracts of such master of the vessel? This depends upon the fact whether the father or master knew, and expressly, or by implication, *approved* of the transaction; or merely *knew* of the same, without assenting to it. In the first case, the father or master is liable to *the whole extent;* for the public good requires that a person acquainted with such circumstances, and expressly or impliedly approving the same, should be responsible for the whole. But in the second case, where the minor or slave employs the ship *without the approbation* of the father or master, he is not responsible for the whole, but only to the extent of the inheritable share of the minor, or *peculium* of the slave. (*m*)

(*m*) This note relates to a curious, but now useless question of the ancient Roman law, which arose entirely out of the manners and customs of the Roman people. Further inquiries of the curious on the subject may be gratified by turning to the 14th book of the *Digests, title* 1. *De Exercitoriâ actione,* which we

E

NOTE XXVI.

If there be several owners of a vessel, they are jointly and severally liable for the engagements and all other acts of the master appointed by them; for a person contracting with *one* should not be compelled to sue *several*. It is otherwise if several owners command the vessel themselves; in that case every one is liable for his own act, nor is one responsible for the rest. But if several owners concur in appointing one master, each owner is liable to the full extent of his contracts. With this principle *John de Hevia agrees in Cur Phil. lib. 3. cap. 4. n. 24.*

On the same principle, any one of several partners may make sale of partnership goods.

Quoted in *Abbott*, 79.

NOTE XXVII.

Persons contracting with the master of a ship, have their election to proceed either against the mas-

understand is to appear in an English translation in the next number of the American Law Journal, edited by John E. Hall, Esq. of Baltimore; a work which contains much useful and interesting matter on a variety of legal subjects, and is therefore highly worthy of the patronage of the practical, as well as the scientific lawyer.

ter, or the owner, for the *amount due*, and the payment of one will discharge the other. The judgment against one of them will be valid either for or against the other, even though the latter had no notice of the trial or of the suit brought.

But if the parties bring their action against one, without *protestation* as to the other, they cannot afterwards proceed against the latter.

The owner of the vessel has no right of action against persons contracting with the master, but must proceed against the master appointed by himself. *Dig. lib.* 14. *tit.* 1. *de Exerc. act. l.* 1. § *est autem.* (*n*)

Quoted in *Abbott*, 79.

(*n*) Our author appears to have fallen into an error here, and lays down his position too broadly. The text of the civil law to which he refers, is not the *first*, but the 18th law of the title *De Exercitoriâ actione*, and does not begin with the words *est autem*, but *sed ex contrario*. It merely says that the *actio exercitoria* is not given to the owners of vessels against those who contract with the master, *because*, says that law, *they do not want the aid of that* EXTRAORDINARY REMEDY. But it does not follow that they cannot proceed by an *ordinary action* for the breach of such contracts, and that they must in all cases be driven to sue the master, *merely because they appointed him.* Such a law would be manifestly unjust, and contrary to the spirit of the Roman system of jurisprudence. See Note LXV.

NOTE XXVIII.

If the master of a ship die, or the slave who has the command be sold, the owner will still be liable for their contracts. This is true, even if the slave should die. And this action survives, as well for, as against, the heirs of the party. (*o*) The obligation entered into with the master is not extinguished even by a new obligation or security, substituted by the master for the further benefit of the creditor who had contracted with him; unless it be so expressly declared. *Dig. lib.* 14. *tit.* 3. *l.* 13. § 1. *John de Hevia, lib.* 3. *c.* 4. *No.* 24.

Quoted in *Abbott*, 79.

NOTE XXIX.

Contracts made by the master of the vessel are *executory*, not only as they respect matters *expressed* therein, but with regard also to every thing *implied*. For on these occasions every thing that may be *understood*, is considered as if *expressed*. (*p*)

(*o*) This relates to the peculiar forms of proceedings among the Romans, which the Italians have in a great degree preserved: but it is no otherwise interesting to us than as it exhibits a view of the judiciary system of that people.

(*p*) Mercantile contracts are generally made *bonâ fide*, and in

NOTE XXX.

If the master or sailors ship a larger cargo than is proper, they are considered in fault, and are liable

their formation it is impossible to forsee every case, and to anticipate every exception. It is highly proper therefore, that a party should not be too strictly bound by a general expression, but that he should be allowed the benefit of exceptions provided by law in similar cases; for the law must be taken to be a part of every contract, in the same manner as if it were literally inserted therein, unless it be expressly derogated from. If, for example, therefore, a master of a vessel has stipulated in a charter-party, for a certain freight to be paid to him on the delivery of the goods at the port to which he is bound, and the vessel is wrecked in the course of the voyage, it would seem that the provision which the law has made for such a case ought to be considered as inserted: viz. that he shall have freight *pro rata itineris*. *Luke et al.* v. *Lyde*, 2 *Burr.* 889. Infra Note LXXXI. For he ought not to be supposed to have waived the benefit of that exception, unless he had renounced it in express terms. The general expression, that "freight shall be paid on the delivery of the goods," can mean nothing but what the law had said before; for in general, and where there is no written contract, freight is not payable until the goods are delivered, except in particular cases, which the law has foreseen and provided for, to enumerate which would require almost a volume in every charter-party. It seems proper therefore, to consider them implied, not only on *equitable*, but on *strictly legal* principles. Yet it has been determined otherwise in England in the case of *Cook* v. *Jennings*, 7 *Term Rep.* 381. But as this case was decided long after the period of our revolution, it is not binding upon the courts of the United States, and it appears to us highly deserving of reconsideration.

for damages. Even if a shipwreck ensue in consequence of the vessel's being too heavily laden, they
are responsible. *Cod. lib.* 11. *tit.* 4. *l.* 1. *Stracch. de
Nav. p.* 3. *No.* 13.

Quoted in *Abbott*, 149.

NOTE XXXI.

The master of a vessel, for a debt due to him by
the owners, may pay himself, or even another person, out of the proceeds or freight of the ship, or
out of any of their property on board: in the same
way as the owner, when he has been put to expense
or suffered damage by the fault of the master or
sailors, has his action against them for a recovery.
Stracch. de Naut. last part, No. 4.

NOTE XXXII.

The master of a ship is bound to render an account
to the owners of every thing he carried out and used
in the vessel, like all other agents, with regard to the
property of their principals. And if the master, by a
public instrument were bound to return accounts of
the ship, execution cannot be issued against him on
that instrument, until his accounts are liquidated.
John de Hevia, lib. 3. *c.* 4. *n.* 26. For an agent is not

liable to execution unless a settlement be first made, and all his receipts and payments be balanced, and his accounts thoroughly examined: and in the mean time nothing can be recovered from him, nor can he be compelled to pay.

NOTE XXXIII.

The owner of a ship may recal the master, and remove him from the command, even without a cause, and though he had sworn not to remove him. This must be understood however, as applicable only to a master who has not actually assumed the command; for if he have begun to exercise the duties of a master, he cannot without *just cause*, be removed from his authority, during the time for which it was granted to him. A *sufficient* cause for removal is, for example, if the master become deranged, or change his condition, (*q*) or become an enemy to the owner, or prove less faithful than he was before. *John de Hevia, lib.* 3. *c.* 4. *No.* 16.

(*q*) That is to say, we presume, if he should enter into wild, or too extensive speculations, or contract such engagements as would render him less secure, or unfit to be trusted.

NOTE XXXIV.

Expenses incurred by the master to repair the ship, or to furnish necessaries for the voyage, are to be allowed him. These expenses are to be divided among the different owners, as they are incurred for the benefit of all. Where several are equally interested in a ship, they must contribute equally to defray the expenses, since they are all equally benefited; but if one have a larger share than the rest, each must contribute according to his share. *Decis. Rot. Gen.* 85.

Quoted in *Abbott*, 21.

NOTE XXXV.

Expenses incurred by the master, to support or equip the vessel, or otherwise for her use, are to be borne by every one interested in her, according to his share of interest; and the ship's books will be sufficient evidence of these expenses. *Stracch. de Nav. part* 2. *Rota. Gen. Dec.* 170. *No.* 2, 3.

Quoted in *Abbott*, 91.

NOTE XXXVI.

If A., a pirate, own a vessel, with which he com-
mits various acts of piracy, and afterwards sells the
vessel to B., have the persons who have been plundered of their property by A. an action against the
said vessel in the hands of B. or against B. as pos-
sessor thereof, for restitution and damages? It would
appear that they have; because it is lawful for every
one to seize and take possession of the property of
pirates, who are considered in the light of enemies,
and because, by the pontifical law, all the goods of
an offender are liable for satisfaction to the party injured. Wherefore, in the above case, it is said, the
owners may proceed against the ship by virtue of
the tacit lien created by operation of law. But the
better opinion is, that the merchant has no claim
upon B. the purchaser. And the former principle
holds, only when the ship is in the *actual possession*
of the pirate, in which case it is lawful to seize her.
This liability of the property to be retaken, continues
against the *heirs* of the pirate, though not against other
succeeding owners of the goods; for the ship, being

F

an inanimate thing, could not itself be guilty of any offence. (r) *Straccha de Nav. part* 2. *No.* 14. 17.

NOTE XXXVII.

When a ship or other property has been purchased; or redeemed, after having been captured by pirates, robbers, or the subjects of a foreign nation, can the owner recover this property without paying the sum advanced? It has been said that he can; for whoever purchases stolen goods, is bound to restore them to their rightful owner, even though not indemnified for the price given. *Cod. lib.* 6. *tit.* 2. *l.* 2. But the law is otherwise. *Stracch.* (s) *de Mer. in tit. de Nautic. par.* 2. *No.* 18. *Dig. lib.* 49. *tit.* 15. *l.* 6.

(r) The English and American revenue laws proceed on a different principle; the ship is considered as the offender, and may be seized after the commission of an offence, which works a forfeiture, even in the hands of a bonâ fide purchaser. *Parker* 227. *Bunb.* 238.

(s) Straccha expresses himself to this effect, " *If one purchase or ransom the ship or goods of another, taken by foreign pirates or robbers, he may recover of the owner the money that he has paid therefor.*" And he quotes the following text of the civil law. " *If a woman, condemned to the public works for her crimes, be taken thence by foreign robbers, and sold by them as a slave, and afterwards be redeemed, she must return to her punishment. But the public must repay the price of her purchase or ransom. Dig. lib.* xlix. *tit.* 15. *l.* 6.

If the purchaser *protest* that he acts in the name of the owner, and thereupon offers to make restitution to him, the original price, together with interest, must certainly be paid to the purchaser. (*t*)

NOTE XXXVIII.

A fine for alienation, or other similar duty, payable on the sale of real or immoveable property, is not due on the sale of a ship, for a ship is considered personal or moveable property. With this principle *Straccha* concurs, who proves by various reasons, that a ship is considered as moveable property, although some writers entertain a different opinion.

NOTE XXXIX.

This note is little more than a repetition of the last, and therefore it is not deemed necessary to translate it.

(*t*) The text here referred to, is in these words. *You ask an improper thing (incivilem rem desideratis) if you require the price of things known to have been stolen, to be paid you, before you restore them to the owner. Rather take care to be more cautious hereafter in your dealings, lest you not only suffer a similar loss, but be moreover suspected of participation in the crime. Cod. lib. 6. tit. 2. l. 2.*

NOTE XL.

Is the owner of a ship liable for a theft committed
on board? It has been decided that he is. For if a
sailor or innkeeper receive any person with his goods,
he seems to undertake that his vessel or lodgings
shall be calculated for the purpose, and that every
thing shall be safely restored. He is answerable therefore, if a loss happen, or an injury be sustained,
though without his fault. Some authors, however,
maintain that this liability does not extend to fortuitous cases, or losses consequent upon force, or
when the property is stolen, for then the receiver is
not liable. *A fortuitous case* is a theft committed by
night, with force and violence, for that cannot be
foreseen; and no fault or negligence can be attributed
to him who takes the same care of the property of
another, as he does of his own.

Quoted in *Abbott*, 159.

NOTE XLI.

Mariners cannot bind themselves to serve *per-
petually* on board of a ship; for any obligation by
which perpetual servitude is assumed, is prohibited

by law: but it is otherwise in case of crimes, for an offender may be condemned to the galleys for life.

But a mariner is bound to serve when he has received his advance of wages, or has engaged with the master for a certain voyage, and on his default, the master may ship another mariner in his place, and charge him with the expense.

NOTE XLII.

Wages are due to mariners though not agreed for, when the master of the ship is in the habit of paying, and they of receiving them. *Consulate of the Sea,* c. 223. (*u*) Provided the sailor be not a passenger who wished to go to a particular place, and made use of the opportunity offered by the vessel, or a person who shipped for the purpose of studying navigation. These persons cannot, without express agreement to

(*u*) This quotation from the *Consolato del Mare*, in the original, is at the end of Note XLIII. but on turning to the chapter referred to, we find that the quotation ought to have been placed here, as it has no relation to the contents of the succeeding Note, but fully supports the principles advanced in this: perhaps also our author did not mean to refer to the ancient book of the *Consolato,* but to the *Spanish Ordinance of Barcelona,* which is sometimes known by that name. See the observations on Note LXXX. in the Treatise upon Insurance.

that effect, demand wages of the master. *John de Hevia, l. 3. c. 4. No. 35.*

NOTE XLIII.

Wages are due to mariners when the master discharges them, before the term for which they shipped has expired, or when he leaves them on shore and does not require their services. Wages agreed for by the master are due also, if from any accident, he should not make the voyage, even without his fault, and without services performed by the mariners, provided they do not leave the ship without permission granted by the master.

It is otherwise however, when the sailor has an interest in the freight and cargo in lieu of wages; for in this case, if the ship sustain an injury from accident, or the mariner do not perform the voyage, he is bound to contribute to the loss and cannot recover his wages. *John de Hevia, lib. 3. Com. Nav. cap. 4. n. 39.*

NOTE XLIV.

If the ship be short of provisions, and some persons on board have a supply, while others have none, such provisions may be taken from those who have them, even against their will, and divided among the others, compensation being made to them at a fair estimate. If the owner be unwilling to receive a fair price, the amount may be deposited with some safe person, and the articles may be taken by the master's own authority.

NOTE XLV.

If a voyage be promised to be made within *a certain time*, for example, if a master of a ship engage to sail from Naples to Constantinople, within so many months, is it sufficient that the voyage be *commenced*, though the ship do not *arrive* within that time? Some authors think that if the term allowed be short in proportion to the distance, and the voyage consequently cannot be performed, the master will be excused. Others however, and among them *Straccha*, (*de Mercat. tit. de Navigatione No.* 13.) contend that in this case it suffices if the voyage be merely *begun*, although it be not *completed*, whether the term allowed be too short or sufficiently long, unless otherwise expressly declared in the agreement.

But if the ship change her course and sail in another direction, she is considered as having *altered her voyage*.

NOTE XLVI.

The supercargo cannot protract the time of sailing, or alter the voyage agreed upon by the master and owner, unless this authority be expressly vested in him.

Nor can the master be compelled by the mariners to do any particular thing. For this reason he is never considered as acting under the compulsion of the sailors, for he can always command. *Straccha de Navigat. No.* 1, 3.

NOTE XLVII.

If a person have undertaken to carry provisions to a certain place, assuming upon himself all fortuitous cases, of *every kind*, with two exceptions, *to wit*, shipwreck at sea, and capture by enemies; and afterwards the ship be taken possession of by order of government, and the cargo of provisions carried to another place, will such person be excused? If it happen without his fault, he will be excused. (*x*) But

.(*x*) It is a maxim in countries governed by the civil law, that no one is bound to guarantee the acts of his own sovereign, unless he have expressly and explicitly undertaken so to do. On this principle, we presume, a seizure or impressment of a Neapoli-

if there be any fault committed, he is liable for the price of the provisions, according to their value in the place where he had undertaken to carry them: for here the circumstances of the case will not excuse him.

NOTE XLVIII.

In maritime controversies, the general maritime law is to be the rule of decision, provided it be not contrary to the law of the land. (*y*) And when doubts arise respecting maritime usage and custom, recourse must be had for information to skilful and experienced seamen.

tan vessel by order of the king of Naples, is held by our author not to come within the general guarantee of *all fortuitous events*, though it would be otherwise if the seizure were made by a foreign prince.

(*y*) A certain *Eudæmon* of *Nicomedia*, preferred his petition to the emperor *Antoninus*, in these words. " *May it please the emperor; Having been shipwrecked on the coast of Italy, the revenue officers from the Cyclades islands seized our property and plundered us of every thing.*" The emperor answered: " I am, it is true, the sovereign of the world, but the law is the sovereign of the sea; let this matter be determined by the Rhodian maritime law, so far as it is not opposed to our own." A like answer was given by the emperor *Augustus. Dig. lib.* xiv. *tit.* 2. *De lege Rhodia de jactu, law* 9. Αξίωσις.

G

NOTE XLIX.

When a ship is chartered to two persons, the first is to be preferred. But if the ship be already laden by the second, or if actual possession, or the charter party be delivered to him, he will be preferred.

If a person charter a vessel to carry his person or goods to a certain place, he may underlet her to another for the same voyage, if it be not forbidden by the original charter party. *John de Hevia, lib.* 3. *c.* 5. *No.* 9.

If a controversy arise among several owners of a vessel, respecting different offers made for chartering the ship, he is preferred who offers the highest freight, and if the freights offered are equal, the judge will make the election in order to terminate the dispute.

A part owner of the vessel is to be preferred to a stranger, provided he is willing to take the whole ship, and for the same voyage that was intended.

The king or prince of a nation is preferred in chartering a vessel, so that even if it has been chartered by individuals, he may take possession for the public use; as public is always preferred to private good. (*z*)

(*z*) See above, Note X.

When a ship is chartered without fixing expressly the amount of freight, it is usual to pay freight according to the latest charter-parties.

A ship may be let out to freight either by the owner or master, and the contract of either will be valid for the benefit of trade. *Dig. lib.* 14. *tit.* 1. *l.* 1. 2. 3. *John de Hevia, in Cur. Phil. b.* 3. *cap.* 5. *No.* 2.

Quoted in *Abbott,* 79.

NOTE L.

Maritime loans or contracts are not subject to the usual rules of interest, when an express agreement has been made that the lender shall assume the risque, so that the borrower shall not be injured by any loss happening to the ship. These loans are called *pecuniæ trajectitiæ,* because they are carried beyond sea at the risque of the lender. (*a*) The rate of interest de-

(*a*) In English these contracts are called *bottomry* and *respondentia,* the former, when money is lent on the security of a ship, and the latter, when it is lent on the security of the whole or a part of the cargo. In France and Spain both these species of loans are known by the generic and comprehensive name of *loans or contracts of gross adventure;* the civil law calls them *maritime loans;* that is to say, *loans coupled with maritime risque, and bearing maritime interest.* We have no such general denomination, and perhaps it would be found not without utility to adopt some one of the above.

pends on the distance of places, and the nature of the voyage. On a voyage, for instance, from Naples to a port in Spain and back, 20 *per cent.* is paid. From Messina to Alexandria, 15; and so on, according to the agreement of the parties, regard being had to the nature of the voyage and the imminence of risque.

Quoted in *Park*, 419.

NOTE LI.

In these instances the lender assumes the risque of *fortuitous cases only*, for if misfortune or shipwreck happen from the fault of the borrower, or any other person, the lender is not liable. Such is the law of insurance; for when an insurance is effected in general terms, it does not comprehend a loss or injury happening by the act of the assured. (*b*)

Quoted in *Park*, 420.

(*b*) In Italy, and other countries, where the civil law prevails, an insurance may be made in general terms, and without specifying the risques undertaken by the insurer, otherwise than by the general description of *fortuitous events*, the nature of which is sufficiently defined and ascertained by law. Within these, barratry of the master or mariners is not included. See our author's Treatise on Insurance, Note XLIV. He alludes to barratry when he speaks of shipwreck happening from the fault of the borrower, *or any other person.* He means any other per-

NOTE LII.

The journal or log-book of a vessel, when regularly kept by the clerk or purser, is conclusive evidence of what it contains. *Rota Gen. decis.* 182. *Straccha,* 305. (*c*) And the testimony of the clerk though a single witness, is admitted, contrary to the general rule of the civil law, to prove an act done by himself.

son *on board of the ship*, considering all such as the agents or servants of the borrower, for whose conduct he is answerable.

(*c*) The collection of decisions of the court of Rota at Genoa in maritime and commercial cases, which are much admired for their equity and wisdom, is published at large in *Straccha's* work *De Mercaturâ*. It contains 215 decisions, printed on 339 folio pages. These Decisions are written in the Latin language, in the style and manner of our Reports, containing, in the first place, a state of the case, and the various questions arising out of it: then the arguments of counsel on both sides, with their authorities, and concluding with the judgment of the court. The whole is expressed in concise and pithy language, and is free from unnecessary digressions. It does not appear at what time these decisions were given. We find them in an edition of *Straccha,* printed at Cologne in 1622, which does not appear to be the first, as that was most probably published in Italy where the author wrote. It is therefore to be presumed that those excellent judgments were pronounced in the sixteenth century or perhaps before; and in them are established those luminous principles of maritime jurisprudence which soon became the law of Europe, and which England has been gradually engrafting upon her system of common law.

It is held by *Bartolus* and others, that documents
attested by him are to receive full faith and credit by
virtue of his office. But the contrary has been decided by the Rota of Genoa, on the principle that
full faith and credit in such case is due only to public officers, and that the purser of a ship is not a
public officer. *Rot. Gen. decis.* 174. *Straccha*, 289.

NOTE LIII.

When a ship is taken to pieces and rebuilt with
the same materials, is she considered another vessel or
the same? If the ship be taken to pieces with the view
of devoting her timbers to some other use, and the
keel be changed, and then the owner alters his intention
and rebuilds the vessel, it cannot be considered the
same ship: but if she be partly taken to pieces and
partly refitted, she remains the same.

NOTE LIV.

Is freight due when a ship has begun her voyage
and from any accident is unable to complete the
same, or to carry the goods to the destined port?
Freight is payable for the part of the voyage performed, but no more. For when a person who has
hired any thing, is prevented from making use of it,

he is not bound to pay for the use that he has not enjoyed, *Dig. lib.* 19. *tit.* 2. *law* 13. § 7. (*d*)

NOTE LV.

If a ship in full sail, with a cargo on board, strike upon a shoal, the master is liable for his fault, as he did not provide against an accident which a careful navigator would have foreseen. But if the ship be driven on a shoal by the violence of winds or storms, and not in consequence of any want of skill, and the ship founder, and the goods be lost or injured, the master is not liable. Navigators are not in fault if they are misled by lights exhibited by fishermen at night, and supposing the ports to be designated by the lights, fall upon a shoal, and are shipwrecked. *Strac. in tit. de Nautis, par.* 3. *No.* 26, and 32.

Quoted in *Abbott*, 159. 169.

NOTE LVI.

A navigator is culpable if he sail, in spite of wind and weather; for the voyage must be made according to the circumstances of the ship, time and place, and according to the practice of skilful navigators.

(*d*) See below, Note LXXXI.

A seaman is not in fault if he act with due care and diligence.

If the navigator remain without sufficient cause in port, when the season is favourable for the voyage, and the goods are in consequence lost or injured, he is bound to repair the loss. *Cod. lib.* 11. *tit.* 1. *l.* 8. *Stracch. de Naut. p.* 2. *No.* 4, 5.

Quoted in *Abbott*, 133. 151.

NOTE LVII.

The master is also culpable if he transfer the goods from one ship to another less worthy, and they are lost. Or if the ship be not tight and the goods are injured, he is liable for the damage sustained. But if there be no fault on the part of the master, or the goods are injured by storms and sprays, or because the water leaked into the place where they were stowed, he is not liable.

Quoted in *Abbott*, 146.

NOTE LVIII.

If goods laden on board of a ship are devoured by rats, and the owners consequently suffer considerable damage, the master must repair the injury sustained by the owners, for he is considered in fault. But if the master kept cats on board, he is excused from that liability. (e)

If a master change the course of his voyage to avoid paying illegal duties, and to preserve his rights, as such taxes are improperly demanded, and therefore may be evaded without a crime, he is not liable even though loss ensue. *Stracch. de Naut. p. 3. No.* 12. (*f*)

NOTE LIX.

The master is culpable if he commit the care of the ship to improper hands. If the vessel and cargo therefore perish, or the goods are lost from the incapacity of the crew, because the mariners were unskilful and inexperienced, the master is always liable: for he ought to be careful in the choice of sailors, or he will be responsible himself.

(e) This doctrine is borrowed from a text in the civil law which we insert, that the reader may judge of its application. "*If a fuller*" says the **Digest**, "*has received cloth to full, and the rats have gnawed and injured it, he is answerable for the damage, because he ought to have guarded against it.*" *Dig. lib.* 19. *tit.* 2. *law* 13. § 6.

(*f*) *Sed quære*, whether the master can take upon himself to judge of the legality or illegality of a tax demanded by the authorities of a foreign country.

H

If a master suffer the vessel to proceed into a river without a pilot, and from her inability to weather a storm the ship be lost, the shippers will have their action against him. *Stracch. de Naut. p.* 3. *No.* 12. Quoted in *Abbott*, 148. and *Marshall*, 465.

NOTE LX.

If any of the rigging be cut away, and lost, or thrown overboard to save the ship and cargo, the owners of the ship and the owners of the cargo are bound to make contribution for the loss. So if the vessel be driven on shore, and the master make a protest before a notary and merchants, (*g*) a contri- bution is made by the goods saved, for the injury done to the ship and the goods lost, and freight is paid.

Quoted in *Abbott*, 219.

NOTE LXI.

If an injury happen to the ship in consequence of

(*g*) In Italy and other countries, public instruments are at- tested by two witnesses besides the notary, who certifies the whole. These witnesses are generally merchants, though it is not necessary that they should be such.

the violence of winds, or by lightning, or from any other accident, and any part of the rigging be lost or fall into the sea, the owners of the cargo are not bound to contribute. If by stress of weather the ship lose her rigging, masts, or yards in a river, and procure others in their place, the owners of the cargo are not bound to contribute to the expense incurred; for these articles are purchased rather to refit the ship than to preserve the goods. *John De Hevia, in Cur. Phil. lib. 3. cap. 3. No.* 10.

NOTE LXII.

The master is reprehensible if he receive into the ship persons with whom he is unacquainted, without due precaution: for if any of the goods be taken by such persons, he is bound to make good to the owners their loss, consequent upon his want of caution.

He is culpable also, if he have not shipped a complete crew, according to the nature of the voyage; for if, in consequence of a deficiency, a shipwreck happen and the goods are lost or injured, the master is liable for the damages sustained.

Quoted in *Abbott*, 148.

NOTE LXIII.

If a ship be claimed from a person wrongfully possessed of her, her earnings or mesne profits will be recovered also. *Dig. lib.* 6. *tit.* 1. *l.* 35.

Quoted in the *United Ins. Co.* v. *Lenox, Johns. N. Y. Cases*, 380.

NOTE LXIV.

This note has relation to a mere local usage of Genoa, and therefore need not be translated.

NOTE LXV.

The master is liable for moneys advanced for the use of the ship, and a person furnishing provisions for the sailors has a claim prior to any other. On this principle, the Rota of Genoa condemned the master of a vessel to pay the price of provisions furnished for the use of the ship while repairing, because he had bound himself for the same. *Rot. Gen. decis.* 182. (*h*)

(*h*) In *Straccha, p.* '305. Though the captain in that case acted only as an agent and for the benefit of the owner, still he was held to be *personally* bound. And so is the law with us.

Has the owner of the ship a right of action against those who have contracted with the master, and may he be sued on the master's contracts? In the first case an action will lie, without the necessity of an assignment from the master: (*i*) and in the second case, the parties have their twofold remedy, against the owner and against the master. *Rot. Gen. dec.* 149. *n.* 5 *&* 6.

Quoted in *Abbott*, 79.

NOTE LXVI.

If a master of a ship take on board prohibited articles, and on that account the cargo is confiscated, he is bound to make good the loss to the shippers. In like manner, if unlawful colours or signals are used by the ship, and the goods are in consequence forfeited or lost, the master is liable. A case of this kind occurred at Ancona. The master was sailing

The case in Straccha does not state that the captain had actually entered into a personal engagement, but merely that the provisions *had come to the use of the vessel.*

(*i*) That is to say, the owner may sue in his own name, without an assignment from the master of his right of action, the master having acted for him, and being considered his agent or representative.

under Ancona colours during the war between the
Emperor and France, and in passing by some Imperial territory he hoisted French colours, and was
thereupon captured by the Imperial fleet, to the
great injury of the merchants, although they recovered their goods. The master was condemned to
make good the loss sustained by the owners of the
ship and goods. (*k*)

Quoted in *Abbott*, 149.

NOTE LXVII.

If a chartered vessel suffer shipwreck or other
injury, the charter-party is dissolved, and the goods
may be taken out and loaded in any other vessel.
But if the ship be detained in port for necessary
repairs, or on account of bad weather, the charter-
party is not dissolved.

(*k*) Our author here quotes *Straccha, part* 3. *de Navibus,*
§ 22, 23.; but on recurring to the book, we find no such text; it
is probable therefore that he mistook his quotation, and intended to refer to some other work. In § 25. we find the following.
" *If a ship has been detained and prevented from performing
her voyage by the fault of the master, as for instance, if he had
contraband goods on board; he is responsible to the freighter or
shipper. For it is but justice that he who committed the fault
should suffer the loss.*" *Straccha. p.* 426.

NOTE LXVIII.

If the master defer going into port for some days, to avoid the payment of duties, or to persuade the officers to excuse him from paying the regular customs, and in the mean time a storm arises, and injury is sustained, is he liable to the owners of the goods for the injury? It is settled that he is, because the loss happened, in consequence of his avarice, and not from any accident. *Straccha in tit. de Nautis. par.* 3. *No.* 37. *page* 412.

NOTE LXIX.

The master is culpable if the ship be not secured with good cables, or if she be secured with less care than is necessary. So if the ship be injured in her rigging by his fault, or if she perish in consequence of her being badly found; or if the owners suffer any injury from his malevolence. *Straccha, ubi supra, N.* 49. *p.* 413. If the goods are wet by rain, or if the water injure them in consequence of the ship's not being well caulked, the master is liable for the injury, because it is his duty to keep the vessel tight and stanch.

Quoted in *Abbott*, 146.

NOTE LXX.

If a ship fall in with a pirate, and is taken, whether
is the master or the owner bound to repair the loss
sustained by the shippers? This depends upon circumstances: for if the master were able to make resistance and did not, he is liable. (*l*) But if he could
not resist the superior force of the pirate, he is excused; since it is the duty of the master to make
resistance and defend himself whenever it is in his
power. This is true only when the owners of the
goods are not on board of the ship, for if they are on
board, the master must consult with them: and if
they are not on board, he must call a council of other
persons and consult with them, whether he should
fight or not. *Straccha in tit. de Nautis. p. 3. No.* 50.

Quoted in *Abbott*, 112. 157.

NOTE LXXI.

A ship laden in the territory of infidels and proceeding with her cargo to a christian country cannot
lawfully be seized, even though the goods belong to

(*l*) This is not law at this day. It is always presumed now,
that the master who surrendered, could not do otherwise.
Pothier on Insurance, No. 54.

Jews, who, although enemies of his Catholic majesty, with respect to the christian religion, yet are not actually at war with our sovereign. When a ship is proceeding to any foreign territory that is not of a hostile nation, she cannot lawfully be seized.

NOTE LXXII.

Freight and demurrage are payable according to agreement. If a ship of two thousand barrels burthen be chartered for a thousand pieces, it is evident that a thousand pieces will be due, even though her burthen be not actually so great, for the parties give the law to their own contracts, and freight is always paid according to the contract.

Quoted in *Abbott*, 180.

NOTE LXXIII.

When a ship is chartered *not generally*, but by the barrel or bale, and conveyance is promised for so many bales or barrels, freight is payable for the quantity only that is actually conveyed. *Straccha (in tit. de Nav. part 3. No.* 11, and 12.) considers it clear that when a ship is chartered to carry a thousand barrels, and it is expressly stated that she will hold twice that number, in consequence of which the

I

freighter takes the whole vessel, if she be of less capacity, the owner must be responsible for the deficiency; if of greater, the person chartering her is no further liable. (*m*)

Quoted in *Abbott*, 181.

NOTE LXXIV.

If a ship be chartered for a certain number of tons or barrels, with the expression, for instance, of " *ten, more or less*," this will not render the number uncertain, and freight must be paid according to the contract. Indeed the freight agreed for must be paid even though the freighter should not ship the quantity of goods expressed, but only a part of them. Provided freight be not promised for the number of tons *shipped*, for then it will be payable for the goods actually laden on board.

(*m*) Though there is *apparently* a contradiction between this and the preceding note, yet there is none in *reality*. The former is a case of mere representation, this of actual warranty; in which two cases the law is essentially different, as well here as in Italy; particularly when it applies to facts which both parties are able to ascertain.

NOTE LXXV.

When a particular ship is freighted, and a certain
sum is to be paid for the ship, without regard to the
number of tons, the whole freight must be paid,
whatever may be the capacity of the vessel. It is
otherwise if freight be contracted for at the rate, for
instance, of two pieces for every barrel, for then
freight is paid only for the barrels actually shipped.
So if a ship be chartered generally, freight is payable
only for the goods shipped. *John de Hevia, lib.* 3.
Com. Nav. cap. 5. *n.* 28. *in fin.*

Quoted in *Abbott*, 180, 181.

NOTE LXXVI.

When slaves or horses are carried on freight and
any of them die on board, is freight payable for such
as are dead? Three cases are to be noticed. First, If
the charter-party express that freight shall be paid
for so many men or animals as shall be put on board,
and any of them die before the ship reaches the
destined port, freight is due, because the contract is
fulfilled; and it is a principle of law, that a person
who has engaged to do a particular act for a certain
reward, is entitled to receive the reward, if he has

been prevented from performing his engagement by any other means than his own fault. *Dig. lib.* 19. *tit.* 2. *l.* 38. (*n*)

Quoted in *Abbott*, 179.

NOTE LXXVII.

The second case is where freight is promised *for conveying* men or animals to a *certain place*, and before the ship's arrival at that place any of them die; freight is not payable for those that are dead, because the contract is not complete, by which freight was promised for their actual conveyance. Freight is not due in this case, even though the loss happen without any fault on the part of the mariners; for it is a matter of indifference how the accident occurred, since the payment of freight was conditional, to wit, *if the slaves are conveyed.*

Quoted in *Abbott*, 179.

(*n*) Our author seems to forget the just and liberal principles which he expressed in Note XXIX. If the doctrine quoted from the civil law govern this case, it will apply equally well to that which he states in the ensuing note, on which he gives a contrary opinion. The word FREIGHT, implies *ex vi termini*, that something is to be carried from one place to another. See above Note II. Therefore whenever freight is stipulated for, it must be understood to be for actually carrying the things or the persons shipped, and not for the mere permitting them to be put on board.

NOTE LXXVIII.

The third case is, where it does not appear precisely, for what freight was to be paid; whether for taking the animals into the ship, or for their actual conveyance. In this case, freight must be paid, if they are merely taken on board, although the animals or slaves should die before the ship reaches the destined port. The reason is, that it does not appear expressly what was intended; and as no fault is shown on the part of the sailors, the contract remains entire, and the whole freight must be paid. A doubtful contract must be construed against the shipper.

Quoted in *Abbott*, 179.

NOTE LXXIX.

When freight is promised for carrying a woman to a certain place, and on the voyage she is delivered of a child, is further freight payable for the child? It is settled that no additional freight is to be paid, as the child does not occupy much room, or make use of articles necessary for the voyage; on the same principle as freight is not paid for a dead person: such trifling expenses not being worth notice.

NOTE LXXX.

· Freight is not payable if the owner, from loss of
the vessel, or any other cause, does not perform the
voyage; and if it be paid in advance, it may be recovered back; (o) for if the master does not perform
the navigation agreed upon, he is not entitled to his
freight, unless prevented by the fault of the freighter
himself; as, for example, by his having prohibited

(o) It was so adjudged in the supreme court of Pennsylvania
in the case of Germain v. Maureau, in the year 1787. Maureau
was the master of a French vessel bound from Philadelphia to
Bordeaux. Germain had taken his passage on board of her, and
paid his passage money to Maureau in advance. Two days after
her sailing from Philadelphia the vessel was wrecked in the bay
of Delaware and totally lost. The lives of the people on board,
however, were saved, and the captain, crew and passengers returned to Philadelphia, where the plaintiff sued the defendant
for the passage money which he had paid him, in an action for
money had and received to his use. On the trial of the cause
this note of *Roccus* was read and relied upon by the plaintiff, as
well as the passage referred to in it from *John de Hevia*, and the
case of *Lake* v. *Lyde*, 2 *Burr*. 889. The court charged the jury
to find for the plaintiff, the whole amount of the money he had
advanced, deducting a reasonable compensation *pro ratâ itineris*,
for the two days that the plaintiff had been on board, and the
jury found accordingly. A judgment was entered of course, and
the money was paid. *Lewis* and *Duponceau* for the plaintiff.
Moylan and —— for the defendant.
(*Ex relatione m'ri Duponceau*).

goods on board, and not from any fault of the owner or master of the vessel. *Straccha de Mercat. in tit. de Nav. p. 3. n. 24. John de Hevia in Cur. Phil. lib. 3. cap. 5. No. 22.*

Quoted in 3 *Johnson's N. Y. Rep.* 340.

NOTE LXXXI.

When goods have been conveyed a part of the voyage, equity directs that freight be paid for that part of the voyage on which the goods have been conveyed, and to that extent payment must be made. *John de Hevia in Cur. Phil. l. 3. c. 5. n. 22. Straccha, p. 3. de Navib. No.* 24. When a part of the goods and the ship are lost, and another part is recovered and saved, freight is payable in proportion to the quantity of goods saved, and according to the portion of the voyage performed up to the place where the loss happened. *John de Hevia, ibid.* (*p*)

If the owner or master of the ship pay to the shipper the value of his goods lost, the shipper is

(*p*) On this, and a variety of other authorities, was founded the decision of Lord Mansfield and the whole court of king's bench in the celebrated case of *Luke et al.* v. *Lyde*, above-mentioned.

bound to pay the freight, because he is in the same situation as if the goods had been saved.

Quoted in *Luke et al.* v. *Lyde*, 2 *Burr.* 889. 1 *Black. Rep.* 191. *Abbott on Shipping*, 194, 195. 3 *Rob. Adm. Reports*, 152. *Am. ed. Watson* v. *Duychinck*, 3 *Johnson's N. Y. Rep.* 340.

NOTE LXXXII.

If the master, for a certain freight, promise A. to receive him into his vessel, and to carry him to a particular place, and the passenger appear to have been on board and to have arrived at the destined port, in demanding freight is the master bound to prove that he actually received such person into the vessel? *Bartolus* maintains that he is bound to make such proof; for it is not sufficient that a particular fact is done, but it must be done by the party contracting. *Paulus* expresses great surprise at this opinion of *Bartolus;* for says he, it is sufficient that A. was on board with the knowledge and consent of the master, since he could not have been in the vessel without his permission. (*q*) Four cases of this nature may be considered.

(*q*) When our author wrote, the civilians as well as the common lawyers were in the habit of raising nice and subtile distinc-

First, If the master had promised to take a person into his ship on freight, it is sufficient that he arrive at the destined port, for it is to be presumed that he was taken on board by *the master himself.*

NOTE LXXXIII.

Second, If the master has promised to carry *goods* in the ship, which were taken on board by some other person, with his knowledge and consent, freight must be paid: for it is the same thing whether a promise be complied with by the party himself, or by another *with his consent.*

Third, If goods are taken on board without the master's knowledge, no freight is due as on a contract; for the master has made no promise, and therefore has performed none. But in equity, it seems freight ought to be paid.

tions, where in fact no real difference existed. It was the spirit of the age. But they could not entirely obscure the strong sense and intelligence which shine through the volumes of the civil law. In process of time these idle distinctions have vanished, and correct principles remain. It is astonishing how few of these subtilties appear in the works of Roccus; for on a comparison with the writings of the common lawyers of the same and indeed of a later period, the difference will be readily perceived.

K

NOTE LXXXIV.

Fourth, When it does not appear whether the goods were shipped with or without the knowledge of the master, the freight contracted for may undoubtedly be demanded, because it is to be presumed that they were shipped with the master's knowledge, and as the master is bound to carry the goods or passengers at his own expense; in case of doubt, it is always presumed that a thing is done *by him at whose expense* it was to be done.

NOTE LXXXV.

If a ship be detained, or the voyage prevented, by the fault of the person chartering the ship, because for instance, he had shipped prohibited articles, the whole freight must be paid to the master, as if the goods had been carried to the destined port; for equity directs that the person in fault should be answerable for the consequences. *John de Hevia*, (*lib.* 3. *Cur. Phil. cap.* 5. *n.* 25.) holds the same principle when the freighter does not load the ship within the appointed time, for in that case the freight is payable to the master, whether the ship be empty or full.

So if A. direct the master of a ship to go to Leghorn, where he will receive funds from B. to load
the vessel, and B. refuse to advance the money, in
consequence of which the ship returns empty, A.
will be liable for all the injury and loss suffered by
the master. In this case, proof of the facts rests upon
the master.

In the case above mentioned, where the freighter
does not load the ship within the appointed time, it
must be observed that freight is not payable if the
master ship another cargo, in place of that promised
by the freighter, for he is not entitled to a double
freight. *John de Hevia, loco citato, No.* 25.

Quoted in *Abbott*, 176.

NOTE LXXXVI.

If a pirate or robber charter a ship to any person,
freight is properly paid to him, nor can the owner of
the ship recover any thing from him who has paid
the same, for the owner has his remedy for the same
cause against the pirate. It is otherwise if a person
freighting the ship from the lawful owner, pay freight
to a robber, for then he is not exonerated. But when
he procures the vessel *bona fide* from the robber,

ignorant that he is such, and pays him freight he is not liable to the owner. Yet if he knew him to be a robber, and not the true and lawful owner, he is liable.

NOTE LXXXVII.

The payment of freight may be recovered by a summary process against the goods shipped, or the owners of them, nor should any dilatory plea be admitted, whether the freight be contracted for by charter-party, or merely by an entry made by the ship's clerk. The shipper is not indeed to be heard in this summary suit, even if he allege that the goods have sustained a loss, or are wet, or have suffered other injury, but he must pay the freight *instanter,* and security will be given to him, to refund if his objections, on a rehearing, be found valid. (*r*)

NOTE LXXXVIII.

Freight must be paid within eight days after the ship's arrival at the port of delivery; and the master cannot be compelled to deliver up the goods until

(*r*) See our note to Note LVII. in the Treatise on Insurance, on the subject of these summary proceedings.

the freight is paid. Indeed freight should be paid before the cargo is unladen, unless the owner and the master have otherwise agreed.

It may be remarked, that as the master is bound to receive the goods on shore, or near the land, so he is bound to deliver them at the same place to their owners, at the time of unloading the ship. If a master receive goods on shore, and they are lost there, he is as completely liable as if they were actually shipped; because, from the time he receives them, they are at his own risque. *John de Hevia, l. 3. c. 5. No.* 13, 27.

Quoted in *Abbott*, 161. and *Marshall*, 159.

NOTE LXXXIX.

Entire freight is due, even though the ship do not arrive at the destined port within the time agreed upon: for instance, if a voyage be undertaken from Naples to Spain, to be performed within two months, it is sufficient that the master *commence* the voyage, though he should not arrive within that time. *Stracch. de Navigatione, No.* 13.

Entire freight is payable, even in case of jettison: and it must be paid as well for the goods thrown overboard, as for those actually conveyed. *Rot. Gen. dec.* 129.

Quoted in *Abbott*, 183.

NOTE XC.

Goods are hypothecated by implication for the freight, and preference is given to this debt before that of any other creditor. So it is with cattle, carriages, and things of that nature, for they occupy room in the ship, and are considered as any other part of the cargo.

The master of the ship may retain goods in his possession until freight is paid; in the same manner as a person renting a store, may retain possession of the articles stored, for the rent due.

NOTE XCI.

Mariners, for their wages and freights, have an implied hypothecation, with right of preference on all the goods laden on board. By which right of preference the sailors may recover money previously paid to other creditors; and if the whole be exhausted, they must have recourse to their personal action. This action is always open to the mariners for their freight and wages, as was decided in Portugal in

favour of the sailors, to the exclusion of other creditors of the master, to whom the money, of right
belonging to the sailors, had been paid: for the sailors
must be satisfied first, to the amount of their wages
due, and then the creditors of the master.

Quoted in 2 *Brown's Civ. & Adm. Law*, 143.

NOTE XCII.

This preference is extended to a person advancing
money to convey the goods, or to purchase provisions
for the ship, or for the rent of a store or house where
the goods are placed, as the goods are hypothecated to such person with a privilege superior to
that of other creditors, even though earlier in point
of time. (*s*)

Quoted in 2 *Brown. Civ. & Adm. Law*, 143.

NOTE XCIII.

A person lending money to equip a ship, or load
the goods, or for the payment of duties on the merchandize shipped, or for the storage of the goods,
or for taking care of cattle, or for seed sown in a
field, or for labour done or expense incurred in the

(*s*) See above, Note XXII.

care of an estate, for an advocate, solicitor, agent, clerk, blacksmith, shoemaker and the like, is in many instances preferred to other creditors.

Quoted in 2 *Brown's Civ. & Adm. Law*, 143.

NOTE XCIV.

These privileges are granted to the creditors, for freight, storage and provisions, because the very preservation of the thing itself depends upon them, and because the goods never could be exported, without these expenses, which improve the situation of all the creditors, and therefore the law creates an implied hypothecation. *Dig. lib.* 20. *tit.* 4. *l.* 5, 6.

NOTE XCV.

In case of shipwreck, the master should proceed without delay to the Judge of the place where the loss happened, or residing nearest thereto, and make proof of the shipwreck. Two or three witnesses from the ship, who must know the circumstances better than any other persons, should be examined, or in case they cannot be procured, others will be admitted. This proof should be made immediately, but any time within two years an inquisition may be held, otherwise the master will be discharged. These proofs should be made also without a citation from the owner, who may live at a great distance. *Rot. Gen. decis.* 3. *n.* 17. is an authority to show that the evidence of the master alone is not sufficient.

NOTE XCVI.

The master should not make a *jettison* to lighten the vessel in case of shipwreck, unless it be determined by the merchants, passengers and sailors, previously called together; and this should be recorded by the ship's clerk. *John de Hevia, in Cur. Phil. lib.* 3. *cap.* 14. *n.* 4. Jettison is prohibited of *powder, cannons,* and the like; by every thing else remaining in the ship, even by the vessel itself and the freight, a *pro rata* contribution should be made to supply the value of things thrown overboard. In this contribution are included slaves, pearls, gold, silver, money and every thing else except freemen, all of which must be estimated. This contribution is not made *at once,* but after the ship has arrived at the destined port where the cargo is to be unloaded, because during the voyage it is possible another jettison may be made. If however, any one of the shippers take out his cargo at the time, he is not liable to a contribution consequent upon the second

L

jettison. *Dig. lib.* 14. *tit.* 2. *l.* 2. § 2, 3, 4. *l.* 4. § 2. *John de Hevia, l.* 3. *c.* 13. *No.* 4, 7.

Quoted in *Park*, 128.

NOTE XCVII.

If any of the goods thrown overboard be recovered after their value is paid to the owner, he is bound to restore the amount paid in consequence of that jettison. So if a ship perish after jettison made, and any of the cargo is saved, that part is subject to contribution for the benefit of all persons having an interest in the said ship. But if by the violence of winds or stress of weather, or any other accident, the ship lose any thing, or cast it into the sea, or even if the ship be entirely lost, and the merchants or passengers recover any part of their goods they are not liable to any contribution for the benefit of the master or of the owners of goods lost. *Dig. lib.* 14. *tit.* 2. *l.* 4. § 1. —*l.* 6. *John de Hevia, l.* 3. *c.* 13. *No.* 10, 11, 12.

NOTE XCVIII.

If, however, after the ship has arrived in port, goods or other articles placed in lighters for the purpose of *unlading* the vessel are stolen before the lighters reach the shore, the merchants whose goods are safe on board are not subject to contribution, because the loss did not happen in consequence of any act done to lighten the ship. *Dig. lib.* 14. *tit.* 2. *l.* 2. § 3. *John de Hevia, l.* 3. *c.* 13. *No.* 16.

NOTE XCIX.

If, in case of fire on board of any vessel in port, another ship lying near the former destroy the ship on fire to save herself, and other vessels in port are by that means saved, they are all bound to contribute to refit the ship destroyed. *Stracch. de Naut. No.* 2. *John de Hevia, l.* 3. *c.* 13. *No.* 3.

If a ship belonging to A. be driven by a violent storm against the ship of B. and the latter is obliged to cut her cables to free herself from the other vessel, it is considered as effected by stress of weather, and A.'s ship is not liable for the injury sustained.

If a ship cut the cables of another ship to save herself, and this other suffers shipwreck in consequence, it has been decided that the former is not liable for the damages incurred. See my opinion, and the decisions that have taken place on this subject in my *Selecta Responsa,* **Resp.** 28, 36.

NOTE C.

When a ship is driven into a port by stress of weather, and there unloads her cargo, she is not bound to pay duties or customs in that place, because she came there by force. Nor is she liable to forfeiture. Neither are duties to be paid for *goods* forcibly driven into port. *Sel. Resp.* 32, 37.

TREATISE

ON

INSURANCE.

NOTE I.

INSURANCE is a contract by which a person assumes upon himself the risque to which the property of another may be exposed, and binds himself, in consideration of a certain premium to indemnify him in case of loss.

Quoted in *Lucena* v. *Crawford et al. 5 Bos. &*
Pull. 295.

NOTE II.

He, who having received a premium or consideration, assumes upon himself the risque of the thing insured, is called the *Insurer:* he, on the contrary, who for a valuable consideration, has caused himself to be insured and has paid the premium, is called the *Insured.*

NOTE III.

The contract of Insurance is anonymous; as *do, ut facias, do si fiat:* as for instance, Titius *pays* one thousand pieces, if such a ship shall safely arrive in Asia. Some assimilate it to the contract *locationis operum*, others to the mere *locatio*, and others again to the *fide jussio*. But the most generally received opinion is, that Insurance is a contract of *purchase and sale;* for he who insures for a valuable conside-ration, does, as it were, *sell* his own obligation, be-cause he binds himself to pay the value of the thing insured, in case it should be lost; and the other par-ty, that is the Insured, *purchases* that obligation.

NOTE IV.

The contract of Insurance is lawful; for a risque may be estimated in money. It will therefore be a good contract, that, in case certain goods arrive in safety at a certain place, a certain sum shall be paid proportional to their estimated value, and that in case the merchandize be lost, the insurer shall be bound to make good that loss by paying the whole of the estimated value.

This contract will likewise be valid, although it be *nudum pactum.*

Quoted in *Lucena* v. *Crawford et al. 5 Bos. & Pull.* 295.

NOTE V.

Insurances are highly beneficial to the commonwealth, and to trade in general. They are most frequent in maritime places.

NOTE VI.

The nature of Insurance is such, that if a person who wishes to transport his merchandize by sea or land, and fears that it may be lost or be exposed to some other danger, can find another who is willing to take upon himself the probable risque to which his merchandize is exposed; then he who assumes the risque may justly require some compensation from the owner of the goods; because a person assuming the risque of another's property exposes his own, which is in safety, to the danger of loss: whence it follows, that if the goods which he insures should perish, he will be bound to pay their value to their owner *out of his own property;* and if the merchandize remain safe, he will not be bound to restore the sum he has received, for assuming the risque.

The loss and gain of this species of contract or commerce, depend entirely upon chance.

NOTES VII. and VIII.

These notes relate to some nice doctrines of the civil law, which can be of no possible use to the American jurist.

NOTE IX.

The ownership of goods insured is not transferred to the insurer, but remains in him to whom they belonged before the insurance, notwithstanding the contract: for if they are lost, the loss is the *owner's* and not the *insurer's*. So it is, if one of two co-partners insure his partner's share of the property; for he does not by so doing, acquire the ownership of all the goods: because by the contract of insurance. the goods themselves are not bought and sold, but merely the obligation is transferred, to meet the risque, by paying the price of the goods in case of loss.

Quoted in *Marshall*, 375. 391.

NOTE X.

Where a merchant has represented himself interested in goods shipped, in the sum of one thousand
ducats, and is insured to that amount, and the premium is paid to the insurer on that sum, is the insurer, in case of loss, bound to pay the sum insured,
if he can prove that the merchant had shipped a less
valuable cargo, or none at all? It would appear that
he is; because in contracts of strict law, a false cause
does not vitiate an express stipulation: but the fact
is otherwise; for the insurer is liable only for the
amount which the insured actually had in the ship;
and if he had nothing, the insurer is entirely exonerated: because a false assertion and representation,
when wilfully made by the assured, vitiate the contract of insurance.

NOTE XI.

But in the foregoing case, is the insurer bound to
return the premium, as in fact the goods were not
on board? or may he retain a *pro rata* premium only
for the goods actually shipped? He cannot properly
be said to have incurred a risque when the goods

M

or a part of them never were shipped. It would seem, on the principle mentioned in the last note, that the insurer is bound to return the premium paid in consideration of a risque which never happened. But in fact, he is not only not bound *to return the premium*, but he may even *demand it if unpaid*, according to the agreement: and the reason is, that although the assumption of the risque does not hold as against the insurer on the principles of the foregoing note, yet *in his favour* and *against the assured*, the false representation will avail. This is held too, because the failure is the act of the insured, inasmuch as he shipped no goods, and is not the act of the insurer.

Quoted in *Park*, 371. *Marshall*, 563.

NOTE XII.

After insurance effected, the insurer may cause himself to be insured by another person; and this second insurer is liable for the contract made by the first, and is bound to pay the whole that the first insurer may have undertaken to pay; and this second insurance will be good.

Thus several insurances may be effected on the

same risque, as several securities may be taken for the same thing.

Quoted in *Marshall*, 113. *Park*, 176.

NOTE XIII.

When insurance is effected and the goods are shipped, if, from any cause, the voyage does not commence, because for instance the goods are confiscated, sequestrated, or otherwise detained; can the insurer demand the premium if *unpaid;* or if *paid*, is he not bound to make restitution, since the voyage was not undertaken, and consequently no risque has been incurred? At first view this case appears favourable to the insurer, inasmuch as the difficulty arises not from his act or any fortuitous event, but from a defect in the thing itself, and from the act of the person insured. But it is not so; for the contract of insurance is *conditional*. It may be understood thus: If on this voyage, a loss should happen to your property or your goods, I promise to restore you their value; in consideration that you pay me eight ducats on every hundred: wherefore if the goods are not sent on the voyage before the *condition* happens, the risque cannot be said to have occurred, and the contract is not perfect. Owing to an impediment which arises before the actual existence of the condition,

the inchoate contract is not completed, and therefore the insurer loses his premium.

Quoted in *Marshall*, 563.

NOTE XIV.

If the voyage be prevented by the fault of the insurer, as if he were owner of the ship,* and unwilling that she should sail, because she was out of repairs, or could not get out of port, then he certainly
cannot recover the premium, and if paid, it must
be returned: otherwise the contract would operate
contrary to the intention of the parties, which should
always be attended to. The impediment, however,
must not be occasioned by the owner of the goods,
for in such case the insurer will recover, if the condition *on his part* be completed.

Quoted in *Marshall*, 563.

NOTE XV.

In all other cases, where the voyage is prevented,
as, if the vessel be burned in port, or otherwise destroyed, or seized by the king for the public use,
and on any of these accounts the condition fails, the
premium cannot be demanded, and if paid, must be

* This evidently relates to an insurance on *goods*, shipped on
board of a vessel belonging to the insurers.

returned, as the failure cannot be imputed to one party more than to the other.

Quoted in *Marshall*, 564. *Park*, 371.

NOTE XVI.

Insurance on the *ship*, simply, must undoubtedly mean *the body of the ship*, and not the goods on board; and, on the other hand, when *goods only* are insured, the ship is not included, unless it be otherwise understood. For instance, when a person owning only the goods, says, he wishes to insure *such a ship load of goods*, (*a*) he certainly does not intend to insure the ship, for it is not his property, but *the goods only*. So if the owner of the vessel, who has no goods, insure *the ship*, he does not seem to contemplate an insurance of the goods. But if the owner of the ship and the owner of the goods be one and the same person, and he insure *the ship*, he appears to mean an insurance *on both*. (*b*)

Quoted in *Marshall*, 227. *Park*, 52.

(*a*) *Illam navem mercium.* This difficulty arises entirely out of the ambiguity of the Latin idiom, in which the expression *a ship of goods* is used for a *ship load* or *cargo* of goods, in the same manner as we say in English a *bottle of wine* or a *hogshead of brandy.*

(*b*) This depends entirely on the idiom of the language in which the insurance is made.

NOTE XVII.

When a person insures *goods shipped* in a par.
ticular vessel, he is understood to insure *money*,
gold, *silver*, *precious stones*, *pearls*, and *rings*, that
are in the vessel; all of which are comprehended
in the terms *goods shipped*, although not expressly
named. (*c*)

Quoted in *Marshall*, 227. *Park*, 22. *Lex Mercatoria Americ.* 268.

NOTE XVIII.

Insurance was effected on the body of a ship, her
tackle, apparel, and freight, during the whole of
the voyage that she was to make from Messana to
Sicily, and thence to Leghorn or Genoa. The
insurers are not bound in case of accidents, unless
they happened on the voyage contracted for and
were comprehended in the insurance: as well because the *acts* of the p rties cannot operate beyond
their intention, as because the words of the contract
are to be most attentively considered.

Quoted in *Marshall*, 161. *Park*, 30. *Lex Mercatoria Americ.* 265.

(*c*) Provided, it is supposed, they are shipped as merchandize.

NOTE XIX.

Insurance *for the voyage* of a particular ship, means her first voyage only, and no other; so where a ship is insured generally, it is intended for one voyage only, unless otherwise expressed.

NOTE XX.

If the vessel, in the foregoing case, change her destination, or begin a second voyage, or undertake to convey other goods to another place, the insurers for the first voyage are no longer bound. For when a vessel turns aside from her original intention, she is said to have altered her destination and made another voyage, and the first is said to be changed. This is the case even where the second voyage is only *begun,* although it is not *completed.* A deviation however from a just cause is an exception to this principle.

Quoted in *Marshall,* 406. and 3 *Cranch,* 378.
Maritime Insurance Company of Alexandria
v. *Tucker.*

and under bills of lading: it is otherwise if they were only a part of the baggage of the insured, unless expressly mentioned in the policy.

NOTE XXI.

An insurance, however general in its terms, does
not include prohibited articles. And when the owner
of the goods ships such prohibited articles, in consequence of which a loss ensues, of the ship, the
goods or other property—or if the owner causes the
ship to sail to prohibited places, or if he do not pay
the customs or other maritime dues: in all these
cases the insurer is not bound.

Quoted in *Marshall*, 49, 123. *Park*, 244.

NOTE XXII.

So where a loss of the articles insured is consequent upon the act or fault of the insured himself,
even if the loss were accidental, still the insurer is
not liable: as if the goods on board of a vessel are
seized for some illegal act committed by the owner,
or those employed by him. (*d*) For when a misfor-

(*d*) *Pro represaliis domini assecurati vel suæ gentis.* These
words literally translated, would seem to mean that the underwriters are discharged if the property insured be captured *by
way of reprisals against the owner or his people*, which would
be perfectly absurd and unintelligible. But our author refers to
the law *cum proponas* of the code *De Nautico fænore. Cod. lib.* 4.
tit. 33. *l.* 3. by which his meaning is fully explained as we have

tune happens by the fault of him to whom indemnity was promised, the person promising indemnity
is not bound.

NOTE XXIII.

But if a loss happen, not through the means of
the assured, or the owner of the goods, but of some
third person, in consequence, for instance, of a fault
committed by the master of the vessel and the mariners, will the insurer be exonerated? He will not:
for the act of a third person cannot interfere with
the obligation; and even if the loss happen altogether
by the fault of a stranger, yet by the very words of
the contract the insurer undertakes to indemnify
against every possible risque.

NOTE XXIV.

A thing lent may be insured by the borrower for
the interest of the owner: and a *deposit* may be insured by the person with whom it is deposited. In
both cases, neither the thing lent nor the deposit
becomes the property of the holder, unless it be so

expressed it. The word *reprisal* (*represaglia*), is probably used
in the Italian language for every kind of seizure with a view to
confiscation, and is not limited to the specific meaning that it
has with us.

N

expressly declared, and the deposit consist of ready money. In like manner *a thing hired*, if insured by the taker, (*e*) does not become his property: for in these cases, neither the thing lent, the deposit, nor the thing hired, is transferred by the insurance; but the *obligation* only of paying the value, if the thing lent, the deposit, or the thing hired, should be lost.

NOTE XXV.

Money also may be insured, and the insurer will acquire no property in it. So likewise where a person insures a ship laden with money, or where a copartner insures his own share of money with which a ship is laden, the *ownership* of the money is not affected. For by this kind of insurance the *money* is not transferred, but only the *obligation* by which the insurers bind themselves to pay if the money be lost. It is the same where one person puts money into a copartnership, and the other labour, and the latter insures the money of his copartner and receives a considera-

(*e*) There are two parties to a contract of *hiring*, the one who *gives*, and the other, who *takes* to hire. To avoid ambiguity we distinguish the former party by the denomination of the *giver*, and the latter by that of the *taker*. We hope we shall be excused for this trifling innovation, which may not perhaps be without its use.

tion for that insurance. Still the partner insuring does not become the *owner of the money*, because in the contract of insurance *the thing itself* is not transferred, as has been said before; but the insurer merely binds himself to pay the money in case of loss; and if goods are purchased with that money, they are the property of both partners.

NOTE XXVI.

If a depositary insure money deposited, having undertaken the care of that money, which was received in a bag, or under seal, this insurance does not make it a loan, nor is he liable for the risk. The reason is, because the depositary cannot use the money at pleasure, but is bound to restore it as it was received. It is otherwise where money is deposited with an agreement that the bailee shall indemnify the bailor against risk, and that he may use it as he pleases; for then the deposit becomes a loan, and is in fact the property of the receiver, which he may appropriate to any use he thinks proper.

NOTE XXVII.

For an injury to ship or goods, by the act or fault of a third person, the assured may proceed against that third person to recover damages for the injury occasioned by his fault. But when the insured will not proceed against that person who caused the injury, the insurer is bound to do so, because he has assumed the risque. But will not the assured, by proceeding against this third person, prejudice himself with the insurer, so that, if he fail there, he is precluded from further recourse as to the insurer? It may appear at first view, that he will; for the insurer is said to be liable only *secondarily:* but it is not so; for the insured pays the estimated value of the risque to the insurer, who is therefore not only liable *secondarily*, but *principally*.

Quoted in *Marshall*, 443, 444.

NOTE XXVIII.

On a particular voyage, if goods are transferred from one ship to another, and both vessels are lost, the insurer is bound by the risque he has assumed. But if only the ship *to* which the goods are transferred be lost, then the terms of the contract are to be considered, in which, if it be said, that the goods are insured on board of *such a ship*, the insurer is not liable, because the ship is specified in the contract; and this, because the risques are not equal in different vessels, a circumstance much thought of by insurers.

If insurance be effected on one vessel, and the goods are afterwards laden in another, the insurers are not liable.

Quoted in *Marshall*, 220. 371. *Park*, 291.

NOTE XXIX.

If insurance be made on things that consist in *number*, *weight*, or *measure*, without specifying the precise number, weight, or measure, the indemnity promised is not binding; because the parties intended to contract for a certain thing, and if that do not appear, the insurance is void for uncertainty. When insurance is made on one of several parcels of goods of the same denomination but of different value without specifying the precise parcel meant to be insured, then the insurer has his election in case of loss to pay the value of either of the parcels; and he preserves this right of election until he has actually paid. (*f*)

(*f*) The text of our author here is rather obscure, and we do not pretend to give a literal translation of it, but we are sure, we have preserved his meaning; because he states the doctrine laid down in this note, to be that which is expressed by the celebrated Spanish writer *John de H via*, in *Curia Philipica*, *book* 3. *chap.* 14. § 10. founded on the decision of the *Digest*, *lib.* 45. *tit.* 1. *De verborum obligationibus. Law* 106. *Qui ex plu-*

NOTE XXX.

If goods are lost in a lighter when the vessel is unloading, are the insurers liable? If the *ship* be specified in the contract, a *lighter* is not contemplated; and the risque of the vessel does not extend to the boat. In this case however the terms of insurance are to be well considered; for instance if it be said, " I insure you *until your goods shall arrive safely at such a city.*" When they arrive *in port*, they are considered *at the city;* because when the vessel is in safety in port, all risque appears to have terminated. But if it be said " *until the goods are landed,*" then it is otherwise, for the insurer appears to have contemplated the use of a lighter, as goods are not usually landed but by means of a lighter or small boat.

NOTE XXXI.

In estimating goods in case of loss, should we consider the *time when the accident or shipwreck occurs,* or the *time of purchasing* the *goods,* or the

ribus. We have turned to those authorities, by which we have been enabled to express in a clear manner what we conceive to be the true sense of our author, and is certainly the meaning of those to whom he refers.

time when the vessel has arrived in safety in port?
A distinction must be observed where the goods
have been estimated at a *certain value*, at the time
of *making the contract*, in which case the estimated
value must undoubtedly be paid; when insurance
was effected for the safe arrival of the goods at Rome,
without any valuation in the policy, (*g*) then the value of the goods at Rome is to be paid; and where
the contract is simply to pay the value of the goods
in case of loss, then the time of entering into the
obligation is to be considered, and according to the
then existing value should the estimate be made.
Thus the damage sustained by the assured in case
of loss is not considered a source of profit.

Quoted in *Marshall,* 78, 533.

NOTE XXXII.

But where the owner of the goods has estimated
them at a thousand pieces, and they were in fact of
less value, is the insurer liable in case of loss *for the
estimated value?* Here a like distinction should be
observed. For it may be covenanted *"If my goods
are lost, you will pay me one thousand pieces."* In

(*g*) We have added the words in italics, in order to express
more clearly the obvious meaning of our author.

which case no doubt can exist, for the parties have
agreed upon the amount. Or a value may be fixed
by adding, " *which are worth one thousand pieces:*"
here if the insurer be deceived, the estimated price
is disregarded. But *John de Hevia* holds, that if the
estimate of goods in the insurance be greater than
their real value, in case of loss the *actual value* only
should be paid. (*h*)

NOTE XXXIII.

When the proprietor of goods effects insurance *on
all his goods,* and at the time of the insurance he has
on board, goods to the value of two thousand ducats
only, but afterwards obtains goods worth one thousand more, and ships them in the same vessel; in
case of loss, the insurer is liable only for the two
thousand ducats actually shipped, at the time of the
insurance and not for those added afterwards.

(*h*) We have recurred to the text of *John de Hevia*, and find
it to this effect, " when the goods insured have been estimated
at the time of making the insurance, the amount of the valuation is to be paid; otherwise the insurers are to pay the value
of the goods at the place of their destination ; and if the goods
should be estimated above their real value, still the real value is
to be paid. *Curia Philip. book* 3. *chap.* 14. § 29. The object of
this law is probably that valued policies should not degenerate
into mere gaming contracts.

Goods subsequently introduced into the ship without the knowledge of the insurer, are not considered as insured. This holds, unless the contrary be expressed in the contract.

NOTE XXXIV.

When insurance is effected on a ship, her tackle and apparel, if she be captured by pirates, and after being shattered by their cannon and sustaining great injury in her masts and rigging, be then liberated, and the master make for a port, where the vessel is refitted and then returns home; are the insurers liable for the whole value of the ship, or only in proportion to the injury sustained? The insurers are not bound if the ship escape; because although injured, yet the *same keel* remaining, it is certainly the *same vessel;* and although refitted and restored to her original condition, it is still *the same,* for the repairs are made to preserve, and not to destroy the ownership. Therefore the insurers who assume the risque on the *body of the vessel* are not liable while *that* remains; but the injury sustained should be estimated and the insured must pay the differences.

Q

NOTE XXXV.

If a partner promise his copartner, that their ca-
pital stock shall be always safe, the promise is void.
Yet this agreement becomes good, if the partner as-
sure his copartner in a contract of insurance for a
certain premium: for a contract of partnership and
a contract of insurance may be made with the same
person, only they cannot *be made at the same time;*
but the insurance should be made after the copartnership is entered into.

NOTE XXXVI.

Another and a more common opinion, is that
although the contracts of copartnership and insurance are made at the same time, they will still be
good. For a *firm*, may be so constituted that one
of the partners shall sustain no share of the loss: and
this cannot be effected otherwise, than by joining
the contract of insurance to that of copartnership.
And also, since a copartner may cause his share of
the stock to be insured by a *third person*, it may in
like manner be insured by *his partner*. And, further,
since the contracts of copartnership and insurance
separately entered into, are lawful and just, they are

not less just and lawful if entered into *jointly;* for it cannot alter the justice of contracts or agreements, whether they are entered into at the same time or successively.

NOTE XXXVII.

This principle extends so far that money brought into a firm and insured by one partner, is thereby so situated that it cannot be otherwise expended, than to the use of the copartnership; and indeed, if a partner expend such money for any other purpose, he does an injury to the firm and is answerable for it.

NOTE XXXVIII.

If the owner of goods or of a vessel, state in the insurance that he is ready to sail at a particular time, when the dangers of navigation are not considerable, and on that account the insurer more readily under-takes the risque, and afterwards the owners of the goods or vessel defer sailing, until an unfavourable season, as until the month of December when storms are frequent on the ocean, and then the ship and goods are lost; the insurers are not liable. Because failing to depart at the time agreed on, the owner after-wards sails at his own risque. Wherefore, some writers inveigh heavily against masters of vessels and sailors, who are detained in port by women or the love of wine; for if they remain without sufficient cause, the ship is afterwards at their own risque, and they are liable to an action by the freighters.

Quoted in *Marshall*, 253. *Park*, 324, 325.

NOTE XXXIX.

If a copartner cause *his goods* on board of a vessel to be insured, and they are the common property of himself and his partner, the insurance is considered as effected on the goods of the party *actually insured only*, and does not extend to his partner's share, unless so expressed, or unless it may be so collected from the instrument. Yet the other partner enjoys the benefit of that insurance, for he participates in the share insured.

NOTE XL.

If A. give to a merchant of Naples, an hundred pieces of gold, with an agreement according to the custom of Sicily, that only fifty shall be returned if the hundred pieces be lost; but if not lost, that an hundred and twenty pieces shall be returned, it is asked whether such a contract be good? It is said not: because the consideration is usurious: but in reality, *the contract is valid*, like any contract of insurance where each party is liable to profit and loss; and such is the case here, when the Neapolitan merchant purchases goods with the money. Where one of two parties assumes a risque for another and each one exposes himself to profit and loss, the contract is fair.

NOTE XLI.

On the question, whether in case of theft, the insurers are liable, learned men are unsettled and contradictory in their opinions. But we may decide clearly according to practice in the following cases.

The first case is that of theft committed on the seas by pirates and robbers: This is considered a fortuitous case; and as the insurer has assumed *all fortuitous risques*, he is liable in such a case of theft. Loss by robbers, by attacks of enemies, by snares of pirates, by shipwreck and fire are considered in the light of fortuitous cases, and are all included in the insurance. This however, only when no fault can be imputed to the master of the vessel, who may have navigated a sea which he knew to be infested by pirates or corsairs, for then he is himself liable, and having put himself in the way of danger, he is liable for all accidents, except in case of storms.

Quoted in *Marshall*, 422.

NOTE XLII.

The second case is where goods are stolen *on board of the vessel:* for this theft the insurers are not liable; as well because the owner of the goods is bound to take all the care of them in his power, and if they are stolen when in the vessel it is considered as proceeding from negligent custody and not from accident; for accidents occur only in public places; as because *the master of a vessel* is liable for a theft committed on board; for in receiving the goods he does in fact promise that they shall be restored safely at all events: and moreover because the insurers are not liable for barratry and fraud of the master and mariners as will appear hereafter. For all these reasons the insurers are not answerable for goods stolen on board of the vessel.

Quoted in *Marshall*, 158. *Park*, 25.

NOTE XLIII.

The third case is, where a theft is committed while the ship is in port, and at night, by robbers from the shore. It would seem that the insurers are not liable; for these robbers differ essentially from pirates. This however is true only when the insurance is against *shipwreck, enemies* and *pirates;* for those robbers not being mentioned they cannot be considered as included in the insurance. But if the insurance be in general terms applicable to all cases, for instance, " *that the goods shall be conveyed safely to a particular place,*" then the insurer is bound, even for a theft committed by robbers in port, and for all possible risques during the voyage.

NOTE XLIV.

Barratry, knavery and frauds, of the master and commander of the vessel, are not included in an insurance or contract of indemnity from accidents: as if the master should run away with the ship and goods; because this is not a fortuitous case, and the master was appointed in the persuasion that he was honest, like a servant or other person with whom the greatest caution cannot always guard against deceit. If therefore goods are lost by *the fault of the master*, the insurer is not liable. *Santerna* (i) how-ever is doubtful on this point, and seems to think that if an insurance be *general*, assuming every risque, it includes barratry and fraud of the master, unless they are excepted, as they usually are in all insurances; otherwise it would seem the insurers are liable: for no fault can be imputed to the assured who in perfect good faith put his goods on board and had not such knowledge of the (k) master as would make the loss other than fortuitous, and con-templated by the insurance. If however the owner of the goods be owner of the vessel also, the fraud of the master will fall upon him. Hence he concludes that the insurers are liable for the faults of the mas-ter, because they ought to proceed against him who occasioned the loss. See below, note 89. (*l*)

(i) *De Assecurat, part* 3. *No.* 70, 71.

(k) Our author speaks here of *shippers only*, and not of the owner of the ship, who is always presumed to know the master whom he appoints,

(*l*) It appears from what is stated in note 89, that the opinion of Santerna was followed at Naples, contrary to that of our au-thor, which prevails however in England, France, and the United States, and also in other countries, where the underwriters are not responsible for the barratry of the master, unless it be spe-cially expressed in the policy.

NOTE XLV.

If any one effect insurance on the goods of A. by name, *or of any other person whatever*, but does not name that other person; not only the person named is comprehended in that insurance, but also any other person though not named: for in liberal contracts such as insurance, all persons interested in the goods insured, are included in the contract. It is asserted by some authors that no one is comprehended, even if owner of the goods, unless expressly named, but the contrary is observed in practice.

NOTE XLVI.

The insurer cannot object to payment because the articles or goods insured are not the property *of him for whose sake*, the insurance was effected; because a contract of insurance may be made even *on another's goods*. When any one has entered into a contract he is not at liberty, afterwards to bring forward the question of ownership. Those insurers therefore are to be condemned who, when the time for payment arrives, search for excuses to avoid complying with their contract. And on the other hand, when the goods have arrived safely, or after the contract has

P

been entered into, the assured cannot excuse himself from paying the premium promised by saying
the goods are not his.

So if the assured pretend that the goods do not
belong to him, or conceal his own name and assert
that they belong to another person, or substitute
another in his place, or describe the property so that
it appears not to be his, in all these cases the contract continues unimpaired.

NOTE XLVII.

The premium of insurance may be fixed at the
rate of five, six, ten or more, or less per cent. on the
risques of the ship, freight, appurtenances, goods,
lives, &c.: and such contracts will be lawful, for they
are a purchase and sale of those risques.

NOTE XLVIII.

Is local, and therefore useless to be translated.

NOTE XLIX.

If goods on board of a ship are destroyed by
moisture, or injured by worms, or devoured by rats,
are the insurers liable who have assumed all accidental risques? It would seem not; because the law

does not allow a contribution in this case, which may be considered as proceeding rather from fault or neglect than from accident. But Santerna thinks differently, and his opinion is most generally received. He thinks that although this cannot be properly considered an accidental loss, yet it comes under the name of a *general risque* assumed by the insurer, unless otherwise established by custom. And with this sentiment a variety of authors agree.

Quoted in *Marshall*, 157.

NOTE L.

When the indemnity has been paid on goods *supposed to be lost*, which are afterwards recovered, can the insurer compel the owner to receive the goods and return him the money? When the goods or a part of them are found and restored *before the value is actually paid*, the owner is bound to receive them, and the insurer will be discharged with regard to the proportion found: for a person bound to restore a certain quantity of goods is exonerated by their delivery; and it must be remembered that the contract of insurance is conditional, to wit, *if the goods be lost;* and they cannot be said to be lost if they are afterwards discovered. If however the goods are discovered in a situation different from their former condition, the estimate must be made not for the whole, but for as much as they are worth.

But if the goods are not discovered until the money is paid, then it is in the election of the assured either to receive the goods or retain the money paid.

Quoted in *Park*, 144, 161. *Marshall*, 491, 495. *Hamilton* v. *Mendez*, 2 *Burr*. 1201, 1211.

NOTE LI.

Is an insurance valid when effected on a ship or goods actually lost, or at the time safely arrived in port and free from risques? In the former case the contract is good in favour of the assured, who was ignorant of the loss of the vessel or goods at the time of the insurance. And where the ship has arrived in port the contract is good in favour of the insurer if ignorant of such arrival. This contract is always good in favour of the ignorant party; for a false cause arising from a want of knowledge of the circumstances, will not vitiate an insurance. It is otherwise with the party who had such knowledge, for in *his favour* the contract will not avail. Ignorance is always presumed unless knowledge is proved. It is presumed from the distance of the place where the loss occurred, and the shortness of time between the occurrence of the loss, or safety of the property, and the making of the insurance.

On whom the proof of knowledge lies, and how it shall be shown, will appear hereafter, *note* 78.

Quoted in *Marshall*, 653, 654. *Park*, 25, 214. *Livingston* v. *Delafield*, 3 *N. Y. Term Rep.* 52. (In *Park*, 233, this note is quoted by mistake as note 121, and in *Marshall*, 238, it is misquoted as No. 175.) *See Lex Mercatoria Americana*, 262.

NOTE LII.

The risques insured against, run against the insurer from the day *agreed upon for sailing*, even though the ship should not actually sail. And when no day is expressly agreed upon, the risque is considered as existing from the day when the ship actually sailed, until her arrival in the port where her goods are to be delivered, unless otherwise agreed.

But the insurer is considered as assuming those risques only for the *voyage insured*, and no other. And if a ship change her course or be diverted from the direction of her voyage the insurer is no longer liable. This has been said before in Note XX. If

however the course be altered from any just or necessary cause, as to refit the vessel, or avoid a storm,
or to guard against enemies; in these cases, the insurers are liable, although the voyage *be* changed.

Quoted in *Abbott*, 157. *Marshall*, 392. *Park*, 294,
299, 300.

NOTE LIII.

If insurance be made on a thousand hides, and a
thousand bales of wool, and among the cargo there
are different sorts of hides and wool, some good and
some bad, as with the hair rubbed off, or rotten; in
case of loss is the insurer bound to pay the price of
the hides and wool, *according to their better or worse
condition*, when the contract makes no particular provision for the rotten or defective articles? If the estimated value in case of loss be *fixed*, then it must
clearly be observed. But if the estimated value be
not ascertained, the insurer has his choice; for the
owner of the goods can no more demand the value
of a thousand good hides than of so many bad ones,
and indeed the contract will be interpreted in the
manner least favourable to him. See above, Note
XXIX.

NOTE LIV.

Where goods are taken by a foreign power or a tribunal administering justice in a particular place, or by any people, or otherwise, by force without paying their value, the insurers are bound to pay the price of the goods to the owners, abandonment having been previously made to them, that they may be enabled to recover the goods or the value of them from the captors. When injustice has been done by a judge, and by means thereof goods are lost or an injury is sustained, is the insurer liable under a promise of indemnity *for fortuitous cases?* The unjust decision of a court is considered with regard to the parties a fortuitous event, and therefore is included in the insurance. The act of a judge in general is considered a fortuitous event, whether it be unjust or otherwise, and an improper sentence (*m*) is con-

(*m*) In considering a *just* sentence of a foreign court as a *fortuitous event,* at the risque of the underwriters, our author undoubtedly has in view the condemnation of an *enemy* vessel, known and insured as such; or perhaps also a condemnation for some illegal trading in which the vessel might have been engaged with the knowledge and consent of the insurers. In every other case a *just* sen·ence of condemnation proved to be such, must be considered as having been occasioned by the *fault* of the insured, and of course will discharge the insurers.

sidered a *fortuitous event happening through igno-rance.*

Quoted in *Marshall*, 422, 437. *Park*, 78. *Van-denheuvel* v. *N. Y. Assurance Comp.* 2 *N. Y. Cas. in Error*, 234.

NOTE LV.

If ships or goods are unjustly taken and after-wards redeemed by money, is the insurer bound to make good the expenses incurred for such redemp-tion? For example, where a friendly power, under any pretence, stops the ship at sea or in port, and afterwards consents to her liberation on payment of a certain sum, as it frequently happens: or even where the detention is by pirates and by any means the property is recovered. It has been said the in-surer in such case is not liable, inasmuch as the ship or goods were not lost. But the fact is otherwise; for as the assured causes himself to be insured against *theft*, and consequently the insurer would be liable in case of theft, so he is responsible for that which is *ex-pended to prevent* a theft of the whole. Whoever in-curs expenses in endeavouring to preserve another from injury, is entitled to recover such expenses. So merchants, who have goods on board, are bound to make contribution in case of loss by force of storms, or in case of redemption from pirates; and for these expenses the insurers are liable.

Quoted in *Marshall*, 422.

NOTE LVI.

Where insurance is effected on goods laden on board of a particular vessel, and the vessel is prevented by any circumstances from making the voyage, the owner of the property shipped is not bound to wait the liberation of the vessel, or her return, if she be compelled to make another voyage. He may immediately load the goods in another vessel, and demand *at once* a return of the premium paid, because the contract appears to be annulled by such an impediment, or becomes as if it had never taken place. Otherwise the delay might continue for ten years, or the ship might remain abroad for that time, and the merchant would be obliged to abandon his speculation altogether, or suffer his goods to be injured and depreciated in value, which would be absurd: and the insurer would be enriched by another's detriment, which would be contrary to the common principles of law.

Quoted in *Marshall*, 564.

Q

NOTE LVII.

Where insurance is made on a ship, her tackle and freight, for eight months, for the benefit of A. and after that period elapsed, within which a loss occurred, other insurances are effected on the same ship; if A. recover from the second insurers by an executory suit, (a) they may afterwards proceed by a formal and regular suit for a return of the same amount, inasmuch as the thing insured was not in existence, and consequently there was no insurance. Where there is *no risque*, any thing paid in consideration thereof should be refunded.

Quoted in *Marshall*, 375.

(n) In Italy it seems there is a short and summary mode of proceeding in matters of insurance, and other mercantile contracts, in which judgment is given *velo levato et sine figura judicii;* this judgment is called executory in contradiction to the regular form of proceeding, which is called *judicium ordinarium*, or the ordinary judgment. The party condemned in the *executory suit*, is obliged to pay the money without remission or delay; but he may afterwards if he please, bring a suit in regular form against his adversary, in which the matter is heard over again, and in this new suit all the rules and formalities of law are observed; and the burthen of proof still lies on the original plaintiff. See Note LVIII. and LXXXI.

NOTE LVIII.

With regard to the proof of loss: generally when any affirmative or negative circumstance is the foundation of the claim, the party who affirms must make *full proof.* In an executory suit brought by the insured against the underwriters, the burden of proof of the loss rests upon the plaintiff. And where the amount of insurance has been paid to the owner in consequence of a summary judgment, and the insurers bring a regular suit for restitution of the money, in which they assert that the loss never occurred, and that the assured is bound to make restitution, the proofs adduced on the summary hearing will not be sufficient, nor will faith be given to them in this case, but the burthen of proof will still rest upon the assured.

NOTE LIX.

The occurrence of a risque and loss of the vessel or goods, cannot be proved on the assertion of the *master alone,* so as to compel the insurers to pay the indemnity agreed upon. This must be proved by witnesses, although they need not be cited to appear if they can be examined in the place where

the loss happened; for if any of them be at a distance, they need not appear, and their testimony will
be admitted even though it be received by an incom-
petent judge. It is otherwise with those witnesses
who are present for *they* should be cited to appear.
In suits of this nature the solemnities of the civil
law are not requisite, but the proceedings are according to the law of nations. (*o*)

NOTE LX.

If a ship laden with corn be captured on her due
course by Venetian galleys, and carried into the city
of Corfu, for the purpose of selling the corn at a fair
price, for public use, in order that corn may be
plentiful in that place, and the master during the
whole time retains his command; can a fortuitous
accident be said to have happened for which the
insurers *on the vessel* are liable? These insurers cannot be considered liable, for the ship was not captured at sea by pirates, or in war, in which case the
voyage would be said to be broken. Public utility
sanctions many things which would otherwise be improper; and princes, or magistrates, may oblige the

(*o*) That is to say *ex æquo et bono*, and without regard to
nice points of form.

carriers of provisions to sell them in the place where
they are found. Here a risque cannot be said to have
happened *to the ship*, for it is not lost: nor to *the
freight*, for the Venetians generally order the freight
to be paid. In a similar case brought before the
Rota of Genoa, the underwriters were discharged.
Rot. Gen. decis. 62.

NOTE LXI.

The right of action on a policy of insurance de-
scends to the heirs of the insured, though they be
not mentioned in the instrument. In other respects
the words of the policy are to be attended to, and to
be well weighed and observed. For in those species
of contracts the covenants and agreements of the
parties make the law. The words of a policy of insurance are to be construed strictly, and not to be
extended to cases omitted.

NOTE LXII.

Where goods are thrown overboard to lighten a
vessel in a storm, are the insurers bound to indemnify the owners for the loss of such goods? They
are not: because among all those who have property
in the ship, a contribution is made to pay the value

of the goods thrown overboard, to their owner;
therefore since the assured *thus* recovers the value
of his goods, he cannot proceed for the same thing
against the insurers. But the insurers are bound to
make good that *rate* or *proportion* which has fallen
upon the assured in the contribution among all the
owners of property in the ship; which *proportion*
not being recovered from the rest is considered as
lost, and the insurers are accordingly liable to *that
extent.* Where insurance is effected against all risques
except for goods thrown overboard and average on
that account, the exception will not extend to freight;
for as freight is paid to the master of the ship even
for goods thrown overboard, the insurers are liable
for *that same freight*, although they were not responsible for the goods themselves. (*p*)

Quoted in *Marshall*, 468. *Park*, 129. *Reade* v.
Commerc. Ins. Comp. 3 *Johnson's N. Y. Reports* 355. *Lex Mercatoria Americana*, 288.

(*p*) " The opinion of this learned civilian," says *Park*, 130,
speaking of our author in reference to this note, " is agreeable
to the laws of all the trading powers on the continent of Europe,
as well as to those of England, where the insurer by his contract engages to indemnify against all losses arising from a
general average."

NOTE LXII[1].

What are the accidents or misfortunes for which the insurer is usually bound? Adverse and injurious events are termed *misfortunes;* and *accidents* are such occurrences as no human wisdom can foresee. But misfortunes include accidents, and what shall be considered an accident is submitted to the legal discretion of the judge.

But is such an insurance understood to include *all* fortuitous cases as well *usual* as *unusual?* Many learned men suppose that such insurance comprehends *ordinary* cases only, and not such as are unusual and extraordinary; (meaning by extraordinary events, such as have not occurred for forty years before) even though in the contract the insurer be declared responsible *for all cases*, whether ordinary or extraordinary, premeditated or unforeseen. But the better opinion is that such insurance comprehends even *extraordinary* events; and at this day policies of insurance are usually constructed in such general terms, as to embrace all perils by which the goods may be lost, as well such as are usual, as those that are extraordinary and of unfrequent occurrence.

Quoted in *Marshall*, 137.

NOTE LXIV.

Misfortunes for which the insurers are liable, are plunder by robbers, attack of enemies, snares of pirates, shipwreck, fire, and all perils happening to the ship or goods by storms at sea or in rivers, or by force of wind or violence of hail, snow or ice, or from the heat of the sun, or where the vessel strikes on a rock, or runs on shore, or from the wars of enemies or friends, or from theft, or destruction by earthquakes, and the like, and all other force which cannot be resisted. And the incursions of *banditti*, preying upon the goods, have been decided by the Rota of Rome, to be included under the description of accidents and misfortunes. *Decis. Rot. Rome*, 208.

Quoted in *Marshall*, 422. *Park*, 61.

NOTE LXV.

The act of a king or prince is comprehended among fortuitous cases. If therefore a vessel laden with provisions be detained on account of famine by any potentate, and on that account the provisions cannot be conveyed to their destined port, the insurers are liable. Yet some authors have contended that the insurers are not responsible in case of a de-

tention of provisions on account of famine by a
sovereign through whose dominions the voyage lay:
particularly if the loss can be imputed to the assured,
as he might have chosen another course, and was
aware of the danger he incurred: and so they contend
also where immediate importunity is not made with
the sovereign for restitution.

Quoted in *Park*, 78.

NOTE LXVI.

When a vessel is captured by pirates, enemies or
infidels, (who are considered in the light of enemies)
a fortuitous accident is said to have happened and
the insurers are bound.

But if in such case the vessel be recovered from
the enemy, or redeemed, are the insurers liable?
With regard to this question, the first opinion is,
that if the vessel were detained by the enemy for
three days, and afterwards recovered, the recovery
is of no effect, the *accident has taken place* and the
insurers *are bound*. It is sufficient that the condition
once existed to the benefit of the insured, by the
loss of the vessel, even though restitution followed:
for by such liberation the assured should not be pre-
judiced.

R

The second, and it seems the most correct opinion is, that although a ship *be* taken by enemies, yet the capture does not make her pass immediately into their ownership, for she may be recovered: and so long as she does not become their property the risque cannot be said to have occurred. Two things are requisite to confirm the title of enemies to property captured; *first*, **that** the prize be within their limits and territory; and *second*, that it be in safety and not liable at any moment to be retaken by force of arms, and it should be in their possession during one night. This is so perfectly true, that if before the arrival of the prize within such territory, the master of the ship or owner of the goods redeem the property from the pirates by paying a sum of money, the insurer is liable for such sum paid, and not for the whole value of the goods.

Quoted in *Marsh.* 422, 427, 848. *Park,* 70, 144.

NOTE LXVII.

Insurance may be effected on articles, goods, or persons, not only *at sea*, but *on land;* money also may be insured when conveyed from one place to another, and the journey is dangerous from robbers or enemies. An insurance on goods or money conveyed, includes also gold, silver, plate, pearls, precious stones and gold rings, though not expressly mentioned.

NOTE LXVIII.

The custom of merchants is to be respected in marine insurances. When the practice and observance of merchants are notorious, any good proof of them should be admitted. The judges indeed, in such cases should endeavour to inform themselves on the bench.

In transactions with sailors, recourse should always be had to experienced and intelligent seamen, in conformity with the general principle, *peritis in arte standum esse;* and their opinions should always be respected.

NOTE LXIX.

The insurers cannot plead *non numerata pecunia*, (*q*) or that the premium was not paid to them,

(*q*) The plea or exception of *non numerata pecunia*, is allowed in the civil law to a party who alleges that he has not actually received the whole or a part of the consideration money of any contract which he may have entered into. *Cod. lib.* 4. *tit.* 30. But it being frequently used as a sham and dilatory plea, its use has been much restricted among the modern nations of

in order to prevent the execution of the contract;
for immediately when the insurer subscribes the
policy, saying, "*I insure one thousand ducats for the
premium of one hundred,*" he is bound by his promise and cannot object that the money was not actually paid. In mercantile proceedings good faith
alone is to be considered, regard being observed to
God and truth; and such exceptions will not avail,
because they interfere with the faith given to the
contracts of merchants.

NOTE LXX.

Expenses incurred by the master of the ship or
the sailors, by means of which provisions or goods
on board are preserved from loss, must be reimbur-
sed by the insurers: for, by the instrumentality of
the master and seamen, goods are thus saved: for
which if lost the insurers would be answerable to
their full value. The insurers are also bound to contribute to the expenses incurred in repairing the
vessel when by means of such repairs the goods are
preserved.

Europe. In some countries (as in France) it is entirely disused.
In Spain it is usual to insert in contracts an express renuncia-
tion of that plea.

NOTE LXXI.

'There is a law at Florence prohibiting Florentines from making insurances for foreigners, but permitting them among their own citizens. This statute is binding even where an insurer affects to renounce its provisions, for they cannot be disregarded as it is a *prohibitory statute.* This law has relation not only to goods and other mercantile articles, but also to ships and any other subject of insurance. (*r*)

NOTE LXXII.

The terms of an order for insurance must be pursued. For example, if a merchant at Ancona direct a merchant at Naples to purchase goods and ship them to Ancona under insurance, which the principal *believes*, (*s*) may be effected at seven per cent.

(*r*) We have preserved this article, as a remarkable instance of the blind policy of some countries. The British nation makes immense profits by insuring the property of foreigners.

(*s*) The original has it: *Solutis septem pro centenario quod credebatur fieri posse;* by which it would appear as if the agent had been limited to the premium of *seven per cent.;* but that would not agree with the opinion of *Straccha,* who first stated the case, and from whom our author evidently took his idea. For in that case, the agent could not have been blamed for having literally obeyed the instructions of his employer: and on turn-

with a clause that the goods may (*t*) be transferred to any other vessel. If the Neapolitan merchant ship the goods insured *without such clause* in the policy, because he was unable to effect insurance on those terms for a premium less than fifteen per cent., and the goods after being transferred to another vessel

---

ing to the case in *Straccha*, De Mandatis, *in summario*, No. 39. we find it there stated, that the agent had an unlimited power; but that his principal had written to him that he *believed* the insurance could be effected at the premium of seven per cent. We have therefore taken the liberty to restore the text of *Straccha* which our author with this single exception appears to have copied literally.

(*t*) The original says, *cum clausula de non transferendo merces in aliam navem:* that is to say, *with a clause* NOT *to transfer the goods into another vessel. Straccha*, also expresses it in the same manner; but if the insurance were to have been made on that condition, how could the agent be made responsible for the loss of the goods after being transhipped, since that clause, had it been inserted, would have taken away the owner's remedy against the underwriters, supposing that he should have been entitled to it without? And why should the insurers have demanded fifteen *per cent.* for underwriting a policy with a clause that imposed so great a restriction on the insured, while they were willing to insure for seven per cent. *without it?* All this appears to us perfectly unintelligible; we are induced therefore to believe that there is some mistake both in the texts of *Straccha*, and our author, and that the clause was intended to give *permission* to the assured to tranship the goods, not to restrain them from it; and we have taken the liberty to express it accordingly.

are lost, is the merchant of Naples responsible for the loss? It has been said that he is not: but Straccha is of opinion that he *is* liable, because he disregarded the terms of his authority. *Straccha, de Mercat. tit. mandat. No.* 39. When the order is without limitation the insurance may be made according to custom.

NOTE LXXIII.

A wager or insurance among merchants of any sum is valid like any other wager when not made on an improper consideration. For if a wager have an honest and lawful consideration, where, from the uncertainty and doubtfulness of the event, one party may gain and the other lose, the contract is valid, from the nature of the thing. It is lawful too for the parties to a wager to deposit the pledge with a third person, that it may be paid over to the winner. These wagers are frequent in Spain, under the name of *Apuestas.*

NOTE LXXIV.

The life of a man may be insured. For example, *if such a person* die in the course of this year, you promise to pay me ten pieces, if he do not die I promise to pay you one hundred. This kind of in-

surance has been decided at Florence to be valid.
Again, the person of A. may be insured *safe* and
free from harm, who is about to pass through places
where there are heretics, Turks, enemies and robbers. A life also or survivorship may be insured for
any particular time. An insurance is considered valid though effected on the life of *one person*, to the
benefit of another.

Quoted in *Park*, 430.

NOTE LXXV.

A person lending money to one sailing or going
to a market, may assume upon himself the risque
of the money lent and receive a premium from the
borrower, without being guilty of usury. It is otherwise however when the money is loaned *after* the
contract for insurance is entered into. Insurance
may be effected on money conveyed through dangerous places, infested by enemies or robbers, and
a premium may be demanded from the borrower to
the use of the lender according to the nature of the
risque incurred. If there were no risque it would
be usury.

NOTE LXXVI.

A third person, in the foregoing case, may insure the loan without any danger of usury, and he may undertake that the money lent shall be restored; for what has been said with regard to the lender, does not hold as to a third person, on whom no suspicion of usury can rest.

NOTE LXXVII.

A *security* also, for the risque he incurs, may demand a premium; as he is not bound to expose himself to loss for nothing. This is not usury, for it is received on account of the risque: and among merchants *two per cent*. are usually paid to a security. This is done also in matters of exchange, where the risque of the person remitting or paying money by the direction of another may be estimated in value.

NOTE LXXVIII.

On whom does proof rest of the knowledge which the assured possessed of a loss before effecting the insurance? *On the insurer:* because, knowledge in that case implies fraud, and fraud is never to be

S

presumed: and because it must either appear from the confession of the assured himself, or be proved by witnesses. In an *executory suit*, (*u*) however, the insurers are not admitted to prove that knowledge in order to avoid payment of the money, but only in an *ordinary judgment*, after they have paid the amount. (*x*)

If in the course of the executory proceeding this knowledge of the assured *appear*, from the documents themselves which are before the court, or the confession of the party, payment of the insurance will not be adjudged.

This *knowledge of the loss* may be shown also by conjectures, presumptions and indications, and even light and inconclusive proofs will be sufficient. The evidence of the *assured's* knowledge of the loss is left to the decision of the judge; and the conjectures which constitute such evidence are drawn from various causes; as from vicinity of the place where the loss occurred, or when public fame and report

(*u*) See above, Note LVII.

(*x*) It would seem by this, that in these summary or, as they are called, *executory* suits, no *collateral defence* is admitted; but that the contract and the loss being proved, judgment goes of course, and the insurer is obliged to pay.

existed of the loss, before the insurance was effected: but such public report should be legally proved.
Quoted in *Park*, 214.

NOTE LXXIX.

Is local, and therefore useless to be translated.

NOTE LXXX.

These subjects of insurance and disputes relative
to ships are to be decided according to *maritime
law;* and the usages and customs of the sea are to
be respected. The proceedings are to be according
to the forms of maritime courts and the rules and
principles laid down in the book called *The Consulate of the Sea*, printed at Barcelona in the year
1592, in which every thing relating to these subjects is to be found, and it is always considered a
guide in these disputes. We will in this place therefore notice those of the principles laid down in that
book which are of most frequent use.

NOTE LXXXI.

The rules and principles of the *Consulate of the Sea*, (*y*) which are of most frequent occurrence with regard to insurances, are these.

The *insured* is to participate in the risque of the thing insured to the amount of *one eighth part* of its value, otherwise the insurance will be void: (*z*)

(*y*) Our author does not mean here the celebrated book called *Il Consolato del Mare*, so well known to every student of maritime and commercial jurisprudence. For when that book was written, the contract of insurance was not in use, and hence there is not to be found a single word upon that subject in the work. But the book he speaks of is a Spanish work under the same title, otherwise called The Ordinance or the *Chapters* (*los Capitulos*) of Barcelona. It contains in substance, says *M. Groult* (*Discours sur le Droit Maritime*, page 15,) the rules and principles of the ancient *Consulate*, to which have been added particular ordinances, concerning insurance, captures at sea, and other maritime subjects. In 1655, when our author published this work, the kingdom of Naples where he resided was under the dominion of Spain, and the Spanish laws were in force there.

(*z*) This rule has been adopted by the policy of many countries in order to interest the assured in the preservation of the property insured, and check by that means the frauds which they might commit against the insurers. By the French ordinance the insured, when they are owners of the vessel or sail on board of her, are to run the risque of one tenth of the whole amount insured. *Ord. de la Mer, book 3. tit. 6. art. 19.* And in other cases, unless they expressly declare in the policy that they

therefore the insurers in such case are not bound to pay the amount in case of loss, nor to restore the premium paid. Nor is it in the power of the insurer to waive this condition, *to wit*, the participation of the assured, and his undertaking for the eighth part of the risque. And if the contract be expressed differently it is null and void. *Cap.* 15. *d. tit. of Insurance.* Yet at this day it seems customary, in contracts of insurance, always to relinquish such participation, to the amount of one eighth, and the insurers bind themselves to pay the amount without regard to such participation.

NOTE LXXXII.

If a ship were not laden with goods according to the insurance, or if she did not make her voyage, the insurers are bound to restore the premium paid for the insurance; for this premium is not earned except where goods are conveyed and a risque run. *Cap.* 7. *of Insurance.* This is laid down in Notes XI. and LXXXVIII.

Quoted in *Marshall*, 549, 563. *Park*, 371.

mean to insure the *whole*, they are considered as insurers for *one tenth. Ibid. art.* 18.

NOTE LXXXIII.

When the insured has not paid the premium of insurance for the indemnity promised, he is not entitled to the benefit of that insurance, notwithstanding the insurers may have subscribed the policy; for the *value of the risque* or *the premium of insurance* not being paid, the contract is void, (*cap.* 17.) With regard to this principle it may be observed, that if the insurers have subscribed the policy, and *acknowledge themselves to have received the premium*, they cannot afterwards object that the money was not paid.

See above, Note **LXIX.**

NOTE LXXXIV.

If insurance be effected after there has been fame and report of a loss, it will not be valid. To remove all difficulties and prevent disputes, a certain definite time is fixed on this subject. If information of the loss might have been obtained by land, time is computed at the rate of three miles for every hour, from the place where the loss is said to have happened to the place where the contract was made. If information of the loss must be brought by sea, the same

computation is made from the moment when information arrived at *the point of land*, nearest to the
place where the loss occurred. *Cap. 19. of Insurance.*

See Notes LI. and LXXVIII.

NOTE LXXXV.

The insurers are bound to pay the amount by
them insured, for the benefit of the owners, within
two, three, four or six months from the time information of the loss is lodged, according to the agreement made in the policy. The period settled at Naples is two months, *Cap. 21. of Insurance;* and
during this time it is not lawful to oppose any difficulties to the execution of the contract. *Cap. 24.*
If a ship be not heard of, the period allowed for
making the voyage differs in different cities and
places, from two to four or six months. *Cap. 25.*

NOTE LXXXVI.

A contract of insurance is always *executory* (a)
against the insurers; and its execution cannot on any
account be postponed after the period of two months

(a) See above, Notes LVII. and LVIII.

has elapsed, from the day on which information of
the loss was lodged. The insurers are in such case
always bound to pay the loss notwithstanding the
existence of any objection, whether it be just or unjust, well founded or otherwise. And they cannot be
heard unless they have previously paid the sum insured. *Cap.* 21 & 24. *of Insurance.* In our kingdom
a royal decree under the title of *insurances* was issued the 23d of September, 1622, which directs that
instruments of insurance shall have *prompt execution,* and shall not be delayed by the insurers. In
matters of insurance no appeal is allowed to the
superior tribunal for the purpose of retarding their
execution.

NOTE LXXXVII.

The foregoing principle does not apply to objections appearing on the *face of the instrument itself:* for such exceptions will prevent the execution
of the contract, notwithstanding the agreement usually introduced into policies of insurance. An exception arising from the contract itself never can be
disregarded, since it is a part of the obligation, even
though the debtor has promised to pay *notwithstanding any objection.* The same instrument that creates

the right of action, creates the *exception too.* When a consular decision appears to be unjust, and exceptions manifestly exist, the superior tribunal at Naples will not direct execution, notwithstanding the agreement in the policy of insurance.

NOTE LXXXVIII.

In confirmation of the 7th chapter of the *Ordinances of Barcelona*, wherein it is said that the premium is not paid to the insurers but for a risque incurred, it may be observed, that *insurance is founded upon risque*, without which it cannot be sustained: in the same manner as a contract of *purchase and sale* is of no validity without *a thing sold*. Some authors remark that where there is no risque, the insurance is void, because no subject exists on which *it can be founded*. A false representation vitiates a contract of insurance; for otherwise he would not have made the contract who promised indemnity and assumed upon himself the risque for a certain premium.

Quoted in *Marshall*, 563. *Park*, 368, 371.

NOTE LXXXIX.

The insurers are liable for the barratry of the master and mariners. But at this day it is customary

T

in insurances effected at Naples and other places, expressly to except liability for the barratry of the master and mariners. An insurance was made against *all accidents and risques in any way arising*, without any agreement to except barratry; it was doubted whether the insurers were bound when the master of the vessel did not convey the goods to the destined place, but ran off with them. On the part of the insurers it was contended that they were not liable for the barratry and frauds of the master; and the opinions of learned men were quoted in support of this principle: they contended too that insurances at Naples were usually made with such *clause of exception*. But the question was decided against the insurers who were condemned to pay the sum insured, because the exception with regard to barratry, was not introduced into the policy.

NOTE XC.

Insurance was effected for the *council of Sicily* on provisions laden on board of particular vessels under the name of the *Marquis of Mantua*, and afterwards the goods were laden in other ships, none of which bore that name, and these ships together with the provisions on board, were lost. It was doubted whether the insurers were liable, and on their part it was contended that where a shipment is not made according to the direction given, and according to the policy, and the vessel is changed, the insurers are not bound. On the other hand it was contended, that the insurance is valid when free from all deceit, even though one of the parties be exposed to greater expense and difficulty than was expected; for then the expense incurred is to be considered, and for that, the party undoubtedly has his remedy. But it was decided in favour of the insurers.

NOTE XCI.

Are the insurers on the ship and freight bound to pay the expenses incurred by the owner of the ship, for the recovery of freight? On the part of the insurers it has been said that they are merely *securities for indemnity*, that the words of the contract are to be construed strictly, and that in contracts of insurance nothing should be regarded that does not occur *between the parties themselves*. Therefore insurance *on freight*, does not comprehend expenses incurred to recover freight, because these expenses cannot be called *a loss*. But the rule is otherwise: for the person promising security for any thing, is liable for expenses incurred to *promote* such security; and the expenses of a claim or controversy *are* comprehended under the name of loss. And if the owner should fail to recover his freight after such claim and expenses incurred, the insurers are answerable for the whole freight. For these reasons it was decided in the year 1631, *that the insurers are bound to* make good such expenses.

NOTE XCII.

The insurers are not liable as for a total loss, if the ship be not entirely destroyed. But if by stress of weather, the rigging, masts, or sails, are injured, and goods are thrown overboard to lighten the vessel, they are liable for the damage sustained in consequence of the jettison. If the vessel suffer an injury by shipwreck, with the loss of part of the goods, so that it does not amount to a total loss, the insurers are only liable to a contribution for the injury actually sustained.

NOTE XCIII.

A vessel laden with oil and destined for Venice, when in the Adriatic sea approached near the Tarentine shore, and while on her voyage there, refused to answer to some public officers in that place; she was therefore captured and together with her oil sequestrated, as enemies' property, and altogether ship and cargo, confiscated to the viceroy of Naples. The owner of the oil proceeded against the insurers, who replied they were not liable, since the ship had changed her course and was proceeding in an indirect way to *Naples*. The owner replied that it was necessary to approach the Tarentine shore before proceeding to Venice, because certain persons resided there who were in the habit of piloting Venetian vessels, without whose assistance they would have been punished on their arrival at Venice. In support of this the testimony of merchants was adduced; therefore since the voyage was changed from a lawful and necessary cause, (according to the principles in Note LII.) the insurers were held to be liable. Decided in the year 1619.

NOTE XCIV.

Insurance was effected for the benefit of A. with the clause "*as well in his own name, as for and in the name of all and every other person or persons whom it may concern, in whole or in part:*" and then the goods were shipped, but A. was not named either

in the bills of lading, or the other ship's papers. On
the occurrence of a shipwreck, it was doubted
whether the insurance would hold to the benefit of
the owners of the goods, since they were not expressly named in the policy. We have expressed
an opinion, (Note **XLV.**) unfavourable to the insurers. Yet contradictory cases may be adduced as
decided in the *council of Florence* confirmed by
decisions of the *Neapolitan courts*. An insurance
was made for the account of the person obtaining it
and all other persons to whom the goods might apper-
tain and belong, or who might have an interest in the
whole or any part thereof. This was decided in
favour of the insurers in the year 1613. And so it
has been decided at Messina. But notwithstanding
these authorities the insurers have been condemned
to pay the loss even where the property belonged
to a person *not named* in the policy; as well because
the owners cannot agitate the question of ownership
(as has been said in Note **XLVI.**) as because, when
they assume the risques of goods laden in a particular vessel, it is of no consequence to them whether
they are the property of one person or another, and
therefore the above clause has been introduced. In
the last mentioned case, contrary decisions were

cited, in which the name in the policy was in blank, and *it was proved that the plaintiff had no interest in the goods.*

NOTE XCV.

A ship laden with provisions, mét with several storms as well at sea as in the port of delivery, so that the cargo was injured and rendered unworthy of delivery: the owners of the goods therefore brought their action against the insurers *for the full price* of the provisions. On the part of the defendants it was argued that they were only liable as for a partial and not for a total loss. And as the *subject* of the insurance was not entirely destroyed, they were bound only to repair the injury sustained, *to the extent* that the property fell short of its former value, as they were *purchasers of the risque.* On the part of the assured it was replied that the insurers were liable *for the whole value,* because they could not deliver damaged articles. The courts of Sicily decided that the insurers were bound for the whole price of the provisions, abandonment being first made for their use by the assured. This does not interfere with the principle stated in Note XCII. for in that case the goods were not damaged and

rendered unworthy of delivery, but a part of them
was thrown overboard, and therefore the insurers
were bound only to make contribution for the articles so lost.

NOTE XCVI.

The owner of a ship chartered to carry goods to
Naples, caused himself to be insured on the *freight
contracted for*. While the ship was sailing on her
voyage, she was captured by enemies. The owner
proceeded against the insurers for the whole freight
that *would have been earned*, provided the goods had
arrived at Naples, though they were lost together
with the ship, since he did not prevent the voyage
and the failure occurred without any act of his. For
the insurers it was contended that they were not
liable, since the goods did not reach the destined
port. But the assured replied that a person hiring
his labour to another should receive wages for *the
whole time*, if it were not his fault that the period of
labour was shortened; and when prevented by accident *all the wages* are due. It is otherwise where
wages are to be paid at certain definite periods of
time, for then if the labourer be stopped, the future
wages are not to be paid. But where *one entire sum*

is to be paid for a *definite period*, and that period has commenced, the wages are considered as earned and the commencement is taken for the completion. The insurers therefore in the case above mentioned were condemned to pay the *whole freight*.

Quoted in *Lex Mercatoria Americana*, 288.

NOTE XCVII.

Insurance was effected for the price of certain goods carried from Messina to Tripoli; with an agreement that the insured should be bound to exhibit to the insurers the *entry* and *clearance* of the said goods, *laden* or *to be laden*, and to show the circumstances of their being taken from the place of lading, and of the purchase of other goods effected with the proceeds of these. After a loss, the insured brought their action against the assurers and obtained a sequestration of their property. The insurers contended that as the lading of the goods *did not appear*, and as the agreement was not complied with, of exhibiting the *entry* and *clearance*, the insurance could have no validity, as the contract supposes the lading to have been made, and that supposition should be verified or no obligation can exist. The demand not being supported by the

U

proof of those facts without which no executory obligation could exist in this case, no *condemnation* could be pronounced: Therefore the sequestration of the insurer's property was removed, reserving to the assured the right of proceeding otherwise.

NOTE XCVIII.

Are the insurers liable, where the master of a ship departs without the usual permits and clearances, and without giving security that he will not carry the goods to prohibited places, and on this account the vessel and cargo are confiscated. In a case of this description it was argued on the part of the insured that the underwriters had made themselves responsible to the owners of the goods *for all risques.* On the other side it was contended that such insurance comprehends *accidental* losses only, and not a loss happening by the fault of the master of the vessel, perhaps of the insured himself, who did not take care that the master should depart with all regular documents, and who neglected to report his goods according to the laws and customs of the place. The insurers therefore were not considered liable. *Mata. decis. of the court of Sicily*, 3. *No.* 9, 10.

Quoted in *Park*, 230, *5th ed.*

NOTE XCIX.

A person lent to a certain master of a vessel about to sail to the West Indies, the sum of six thousand pieces, under a contract that *seventy per cent.* should be paid; and effected as security for payment, an insurance on the body of that ship. The vessel was taken by pirates and pillaged, and after being injured by their cannon was liberated as useless to them. With much difficulty she reached the nearest port, the sailors having undergone great labour, and having been exposed to great danger, and was there refitted. The *lender* who was the insured, brought his action *for the loan* against the insurers, who objected that they were not liable to pay because the ship remained safe, and therefore, as she had not *perished*, the obligation did not arise: For although the vessel were *partially repaired*, so that she might be in a situation to make her voyage, yet as the *same keel* remained, she was in effect the same ship. They contended that at the utmost they were answerable only for the injury actually sustained by the vessel on a computation of her value, for the master had received sums of money which exceeded the value of the ship itself. In this case however, the insurers were compelled to pay the loss for the

benefit of the assured: but as the money loaned exceeded the value of the ship, it was adjudged that a
computation should be made, and the money paid,
according to the actual value of the ship which remained safe.

NOTE C.

Insurances effected *abroad* are executory *within
this kingdom*. Because it is a principle of the general maritime law that such contracts are to be enforced by a summary proceeding and their execution
is not to be impeded by any plea however founded.
See the *Consulate of the Sea. tit. of Insurance, art.*
21, 24. and the *Decisions of the Rota of Genoa,
decis.* 3. See also above, Note LXXXVI. And
also because contracts made abroad are to be enforced according to the law of the place where the
suit is brought. Thus the *Rota of Genoa, decis.* 100.
adjudged that a contract of insurance made abroad
between foreigners, should be enforced according
to the forms prescribed by the Genoese statutes.
An instrument entered into, *out of* the kingdom
may therefore be enforced according to our own
forms. It is the same with a bill of exchange; and a
decision to this effect in our own tribunals is report-
ed by *Reg. Sanfelic. decis.* 311, *part* 2.

INDEX.

X

FOREIGN POWER.

How its acts affect the insurance, *page* 119. 124.

FOREIGN CONTRACTS.

Commercial contracts made abroad may be enforced elsewhere, 156.

But the judicial forms of proceeding of the country where the suit is brought must be pursued, 156.

FREIGHT.

Definition of, 17.

When no freight is fixed, what is due, 51.

Who may let out a ship to freight, 51.

When due, 55.

Is payable according to agreement, 65.

How payable, 65. 66. 67.

Whether due for slaves or animals that die on board, 67. 68.

Payable for a part of the voyage, 71.

What proof is required of goods or passengers being on board, 72. 73. 74.

Due, if the voyage is prevented by the fault of the shipper, 74. 75.

Not due if the voyage is not performed, 70.

How recovered, 76.

When it must be paid, 76. 77.

Entire freight is due if the voyage is *commenced* though not *completed* in the time agreed upon, 77.

So in case of jettison, 77.

Goods are hypothecated by implication for freight and this debt has a preference, 78.

Insurers are liable for entire freight, when a ship is captured on her voyage, 152.

See *Insurance*.

INDEX.

INSURANCE.

INDEX.

INDEX.

INDEX.

Liable if he ship too large a cargo, *page* 37.

May pay himself out of the freight or other property on board, 38.

Must render an account, 38.

May be recalled, 39.

Expenses allowed him, 40.

What is evidence of these expenses, 40.

Cannot be compelled by the mariners, 48.

Liable for money advanced for the use of the ship, 60.

Liable if he take on board prohibited articles, 61.

So if he use unlawful signals, 61.

Or if the ship is badly found, 63.

May retain goods till freight is paid, 76. 78.

Must deliver goods on shore, 77.

In case of shipwreck should make proof of loss, 80.

See *Insurance, Mariner, Owners.*

MONEY.

May be insured, and the insurer will acquire no property in it, 98.

ORDER FOR INSURANCE.

The terms of an order must be pursued, 133.

Where without limitation the insurance may be according to custom, 135.

OWNERS OF A SHIP.

Responsible for contracts and fault of the master, 23.

And for the fault of the mariners, 23.

How far this liability extends, 23. 24. 26. 27. 28. 33. 34. 36. 44.

Liable for money borrowed for the ship's use, 31.

Certain things requisite to make them liable in this case, 32.

Where there are several owners, 34.

Have no action against persons contracting with the master, *qu.* 35. See page 61.

INDEX.

INDEX.

RISQUE.
At what time it commences, *page* 117.

SHIP.
The term *ship*, does not include the boat, 29.

How far liable for acts of its owners, 41. 42.

Is personal property, 43.

Of two persons chartering a ship, who is preferred, 50.

May be underlet, 50.

If claimed from a person wrongfully possessed, the earnings are recovered also, 60.

When said to be destroyed, 54.

Not liable if she cut the cables of another ship to save herself, 83.

See *Insurance.*

VOYAGE.
If a ship *change her course*, she is said to alter the voyage, 47. 95.

If changed from necessity the insurers are liable, 117. 148. 149.

WAGER.
A wager or insurance among merchants is valid like any other wager when not made on an improper consideration, 135.

WAGES.
Due to mariners though not agreed for, 45.

So if the mariners are discharged before the voyage ends, 46.